I0820328

HOME

HOME

by Natural Harry

DIY Recipes for a Toxin-Free, Low-Waste Life

Harriet Birrell

Photography by Nikole Ramsay

Hardie Grant

BOOKS

CONTENTS

INTRODUCTION

Home is so much more than shelter. Home is a sanctuary, a space where you can think and recharge. Every little bit counts towards making a home feel nurturing, down to how you care for the space and the people who live there. That's why the home, cleaning and body products you use really matter.

I started thinking a lot about the products I was using at home about seven years ago when my partner, Fraser, and I were operating a small smoothie and raw desserts caravan. The more I began to appreciate how food was grown and processed, the more I wanted to eat food as close to its natural 'whole' state as possible, free of chemicals and preservatives. That passion for natural, plant-based living drove me to question the things I used every day. I was shocked to discover that synthetic preservatives were in almost all of my store-bought cleaning, home and body products, along with loads of ingredients I couldn't identify. Some were known to be harmful. I also learned that manufacturers can get away with a lot by using labels and terms that mask what a product contains. The simple word 'parfum' or 'fragrance' can be a front for thousands of chemicals that are all known endocrine disruptors. These vague labels make it close to impossible for people to truly know what's in the products they're using. No, thanks!

I had read that our skin is our largest organ, and much of what comes into contact with it is absorbed right into our bloodstream. We already avoid spraying synthetic pesticides and herbicides on our food, so why do we spray products that are equally harmful in our homes? Or worse, use them on our bodies? With this knowledge, I began to look for products that were free of chemicals with the power to hurt us and our planet. It was a tedious and often confusing task, made more so by a large amount of greenwashing (conventional and synthetically fragranced products posing as 'earth friendly', 'eco' or 'natural' when they are, in fact, not).

I continued to research, slowly replacing most of my household and body products with things I found at local healthfood stores and online. I was certainly happy with them, but I also knew there was more I could be doing, not only for my bank account but to reduce my consumption of disposable plastic bottles. What if I could avoid buying home, body and cleaning products in throwaway packaging altogether? What if I didn't have to go to the shops at all, or wait for an online order to arrive because stock had run out? So I set about replacing it all with homemade, natural alternatives. That was a journey in itself, especially since I didn't have this book to refer to. I spent hours trawling the internet for recipes that didn't use questionable ingredients or turn your hair into a bird's nest (yep, been there!). But I've found recipes that work wonders, and so skipping the shop and making them at home has become my reality. With this book, it can become yours too.

This book's mission is to offer you recipes, tips and hacks that are accessible, simple, effective, practical, natural and sustainable. I am also happy for the opportunity to save you money and tedious trial and error. I know that making your own home and body products can seem like a lot of work, but once you have the core ingredients you need on hand, your pantry will become the store and you can top up or replace your products without having to go out for them. Within these pages you'll find a list of every ingredient I call for (see The cupboard, page 21), as well as a little explanation about what it is, what it does and where to source it. You may recognise most or all of them. You may even have some in your cupboard already.

My wish is that this book will inspire you to take steps towards less waste and greater simplicity, creating a nurturing and healthy environment for body and mind. It will arm you with everything you'll need to create a calm, clean home.

Finally, a note of gratitude to you for being open to the message in my book. Let's do this!

Harry x

THE BENEFITS OF MAKING NATURAL PRODUCTS AT HOME

- The first thing I noticed about my natural products, aside from their amazing effectiveness, was how much less offensive their scents were, and how much less irritating to my skin and eyes. Pretty soon I couldn't walk down the cleaning aisle of the supermarket without holding my breath.
- The ingredients in all of these recipes can be bought in bulk, and almost all of them without any plastic packaging. Once you get them home, you can store them in glass jars and upcycled containers. That means less waste, which is better for you and our planet!
- Buying in bulk means more convenience in the long run, less waste AND more savings. Shopping this way, then making products yourself with just a few ingredients, will save you money that you can spend on the things that matter.
- Store-bought body and home products, even many of the ones that claim to be 'natural' and 'eco-friendly', are loaded with toxins. Making your own natural DIY products means you'll know (and be able to pronounce!) every ingredient that's in them. You can shampoo your hair and lather your body with luxurious body butter knowing that you're not putting anything potentially harmful on your skin.
- Hoping to keep your body products vegan? Skip honey and use something else. Don't like the smell of lavender? Use orange blossom instead. When you make your own products from natural ingredients, you get to control what goes into them.
- Homemade products are a pleasure to use! Removing the harsh and synthetic will make cleaning and body care a joyful ritual rather than a dreaded chore, and it will help you tread more lightly on the earth.
- Once you've got the core ingredients on hand, bought in bulk, you'll be ready to replace any products as soon as they run out without having to run to the store. And you'll be able to make beautiful, natural gifts for friends and family!

TAHINI
OLIVE
OIL
OATS

TIPS

Here are my tried-and-tested tips and tricks when it comes to making products at home, developed over years of trial and error. They offer ways to reduce your household waste and make sourcing and storing your natural ingredients and homemade products simple, as well as cost- and time-effective. There is a little to do to get started, but it's like a ball rolling downhill: a little push is needed to get it going, but once it's rolling it takes care of itself!

SHOPPING

- Get to know your local bulk wholefoods store. They are your best bet if you want to avoid packaging, as they encourage you to bring and fill your own containers rather than buying things packaged.
- Before you head to the store, make sure to weigh your jars and label them with what you plan to put in them. It will make your shopping experience go much more quickly, and you will get exactly what you need.

STORAGE

- Use durable, long-lasting storage containers such as glass jars, Pyrex or other glass storage containers, ceramic pots, stainless-steel lunchboxes, and silicone pouches and food covers. They'll make avoiding plastic easy.
- Dark-glass bottles (I tend to use amber) help protect ingredients such as essential oils from the damaging effects of sunlight. Storing homemade products in a cool, dry place will also help protect their natural, raw ingredients. When buying a new dark glass jar or bottle, buy once and buy well. Look for ones made from recycled and recyclable materials, and that come with a pump or spray attachment for ease of use. Better yet, clean and reuse amber bottles when you have finished with their contents.

REUSE/UPCYCLE

- Wash and reuse glass jars and containers from any store-bought products to store dry ingredients and staples such as sauces, dips and spreads, as well as homemade yoghurt and preserves. Make sure to hold on to their lids too!
- If you're on the hunt for jars and non-plastic containers, look in thrift stores or ask your family, friends or neighbours. They may have some they are happy to let go of.
- When you find yourself with a jar surplus, fill them with beautiful homemade products such as bath soak, candles or tea. They make very thoughtful gifts!
- Use washable and reusable cloths for cleaning instead of throwaway wipes.
- Cut up irreparable clothing, such as t-shirts you would otherwise throw out, and use them as cleaning cloths and wipes. Just make sure they're cotton or made of some other natural, absorbent fabric.

EQUIPMENT

This basic equipment makes creating simple body, cleaning and food products at home that much easier. Each recipe lists the equipment you need, but here I've listed the key pieces of equipment in one place.

- Immersion blender and/or food processor
- Double boiler (you can create one by putting a heatproof bowl over a large saucepan)
- Silicone cupcake trays and ice-cube trays
- Funnel
- Saucepans of different sizes
- Mixing bowls (glass, metal or wood)
- Whisks and mixing spoons (preferably not plastic)
- Spray, pump, roller and foaming bottles. Glass is more durable and longer lasting than plastic, but if you're worried about dropping glass shampoo bottles in the shower, I totally get it!

- Measuring cups and spoons (preferably not plastic). This book uses 20 ml (¾ fl oz) tablespoons, so if you're working with 15 ml (½ fl oz) tablespoons, be generous with your measurements. As well, metric cup measurements are used, i.e. 250 ml (8½ fl oz) for 1 cup; in the US, 1 cup is 237 ml (8 fl oz), so if you're in the US, be generous with your cup measurements; in the UK, 1 cup is 284 ml (9½ fl oz), so if you're in the UK, be scant with your measurements.
- Scale
- Label maker or permanent marker
- Glass jars of different sizes, with lids

LABELLING

- Have fun labelling your jars and enjoy the eclectic mix of shapes and sizes! This is not about social media pantry porn. This is about practicality and saving waste.
- Clearly label your DIY home and body products with the product name and the date you made it. I use a label maker, a permanent marker or simply write it on a tag and tie it around the top of the container.

WARDROBE

Kintsugi is the centuries-old Japanese technique of repairing broken objects with gold. It is about more than fixing something; it actually makes the object even more treasured and unique. I like to treat my clothing this way too, as something to repair and continue to wear with pride. Some of my most treasured items of clothing have been repaired multiple times, which I believe only adds to their charm.

Carrying out minor repairs to your favourite pieces will not only save them from landfill, but also save you dollars and give you lots of satisfaction. Arm yourself with some basic skills such as darning, hemming and replacing buttons to ensure you get the most out of your clothes.

The following are some ways you can repair or upcycle treasured pieces of clothing:

Knit

Unravel an irreparable but quality woollen jumper and use the yarn to make a few beanies or a scarf.

Darn

Repair small holes and pulls in knits.

Patch

Save some beautiful fabric and use it to patch over holes in woven garments.

Hem

Repair the hems of worn-out pants or skirts, or shorten thrift store finds that are too long for you.

Sew on new buttons

Always keep spare buttons from garments. The next time one of your buttons falls off or goes missing you will be able to dip into your collection and find the best fit!

Use natural dye

Refresh tired white clothing by dying it botanically. The options are endless, and the colour palate is soft, earthy and beautiful. There are fabulous workshops, books and blogs on the subject, and it is such a fun and satisfying project. My favourite natural dyes come from pomegranate, which makes a beautiful, soft khaki green, and avocado, which makes a soft, dusky pink. (I know it sounds strange, but this is what happens with natural dyes!)

Visit your local tailor

Most small repair jobs are straightforward and quick, making them inexpensive to get done by a tailor. You can avoid waste and save money.

CLOTHES SHOPPING

Being conscious about not being wasteful actually begins when you buy your clothes. Quality and make is key if you want your pieces to last. It also means that you are sending great quality, lasting garments into circulation, to be donated, handed down, gifted, swapped or repaired and worn again.

When buying a garment, employ these rules:

— Buy once and buy well. Invest in quality locally made pieces that will see you through many seasons and years.

— Buy second hand or at swap meets.

When you own excess garments in good condition, let go of them consciously:

— Donate them.

— Sell them.

— Create or attend a swap meet.

When garments made of natural fabrics are beyond repair:

— Cut them into squares to use as cleaning cloths and wipes.

— Use the fabric from thin cotton garments to make beeswax wraps for food storage.

CO
CO
NUT

THE CUPBOARD

The ingredients listed here are all staples used throughout the book's body and home recipes, and this section offers a little more information on each of them.

Luckily, most are easy to find in many health food stores, bulk wholefoods stores, some supermarkets and online. You might even find some in your garden!

ALOE VERA GEL

The aloe vera plant stores water in its leaves in the form of this cooling gel. It works beautifully as a moisturiser and a soothing agent for sunburns, bug bites, cuts and other skin issues. Be sure to look at what's in it before you buy, as some brands have chemical additives: look for at least 99.9 per cent aloe. You can find organic aloe vera gel at most wholefoods and health food stores as well as online. Better yet, grow fresh aloe in your garden or in a pot. Just remember that the products you make with fresh aloe gel and juice need to be used the same day, as it doesn't last long!

APPLE-CIDER VINEGAR

When apple cider is fermented, its alcohol is converted to acetic acid, which is the active ingredient in vinegar. Traditionally it's been used as a food preservative and to cleanse and disinfect, including as a treatment for fungal infections. It is widely used in tonics and some natural DIY skin and haircare products. For cleaning, use unpasteurised and unfiltered apple-cider vinegar, and for cooking make sure that it is raw or contains 'the mother' (the beneficial bacteria developed during fermentation). Find it in bulk wholefoods stores, health food stores, grocers and supermarkets.

ARROWROOT POWDER

This starch comes from the roots of several tropical plants, including tapioca. It is used in baking, but also in some natural cosmetic products, as it enables active ingredients to penetrate the upper layers of the skin and promote moisture absorption. Always look for organic arrowroot powder.

BEESWAX

Beeswax is made by honeybees in the process of constructing their hives, used for storing honey. Look for wax that is local and sustainably sourced by beekeepers who only remove a small amount of wax when they harvest honey, leaving enough for the bees to build on. A little goes a long way, and not a lot is needed to create a very rich and nourishing skincare product. It can be found online and at many bulk wholefoods and health food stores. Better yet, get to know your local beekeeper and source your beeswax in your area!

BENTONITE CLAY

Bentonite clay is a very fine, soft powder formed under seabeds from volcanic ash. When mixed with water, it forms a paste that has many cosmetic uses. Its high concentration of minerals such as silica, calcium, magnesium, iron and potassium make it a powerful detoxifier, absorbing and removing heavy metals and impurities. Look for food-grade, organic bentonite clay harvested as locally as possible. Many bulk wholefoods and health food stores sell it, or you can find it online. Make sure to store it in wood or glass containers, as it can absorb metal's properties.

BICARB SODA (BAKING SODA)

Bicarb is short for bicarbonate of soda or sodium bicarbonate. This fine powder is a natural, slightly alkaline mineral with a wide range of uses due to its non-abrasive quality: it's a great addition to toothpaste, helps counteract oily hair roots and makes an excellent deodoriser. I like to store mine in a labelled icing-sugar shaker in the cleaning cupboard, as it makes shaking it out onto a surface that much easier.

CACAO BUTTER

Cacao butter is made by grinding cacao beans, then heating and pressing them to separate the powder from the butter, which looks a whole lot like chocolate but without the dark colour. It's the basis of all quality chocolate. It also makes a wonderful addition to many DIY body products, as it is richly moisturising and solid at room temperature, so holds its form. Make sure to look for fair-trade cacao butter.

CITRIC ACID

Citric acid is a weak organic acid that occurs naturally in citrus fruits. In its refined form it comes as an odourless, colourless powder. It is a powerful and useful disinfectant and cleaner, and I find it a great addition to laundry and dishwashing powder. Many bulk wholefoods stores sell citric acid. You can also find it online and in some health food stores and supermarkets. Look for food-grade, organic citric acid.

COFFEE GROUNDS

Coffee grounds make a wonderful natural exfoliator that detoxifies and brightens the skin. They're wonderful in simple DIY body products. I like to use coffee beans from my local bulk wholefoods store to avoid plastic packaging. If you prefer to use used coffee grounds, make sure they are dry before use. You can dry the grounds by baking them in a low oven for 20-30 minutes; be sure to turn them every 10 minutes so they dry evenly.

EPSOM SALTS

Also known as magnesium sulfate, Epsom is not actually a salt but a naturally occurring mineral. It gets its name from the town of Epsom in England, where it was originally discovered. Full of magnesium, it's said to help relieve stress, promote a good night's sleep and help sore muscles. Epsom salts have many uses, including in laundry detergent, as a mild household plant fertiliser and as a relaxing bath soak.

ESSENTIAL OILS

Essential oils are incredibly potent compounds obtained by distilling a wide variety of plant matter. They are not actually an oil, but a volatile liquid with odours and characteristics bestowed by the plant they are derived from. They are widely used in the cosmetic industry as well as in soaps, perfumes and household cleaning products. They can deodorise a space, strengthen hair, help with relaxation and stress relief, and they make a fabulous alternative to perfume.

It is important that you look for essential oils in their most pure form with no additives. Look for certified therapeutic-grade, pure and organic. There are a few ways to determine that what you are buying is, in fact, unadulterated pure essential oil. If a brand is selling a variety of oils with much the same price tag despite being derived from varying plants, you can be fairly sure they have been diluted with other substances. Different plants yield different amounts of oil and that is reflected in the price. For example, it takes thirty to fifty roses to produce one drop of rose oil, and about a third of a lemon to produce one drop of lemon oil. Therefore, lemon essential oil is much cheaper.

A VERY important thing to note here is that less is more. Despite their beautiful scent and various uses, even completely natural ingredients can be toxic in high doses. For that reason, I tend to use much less in my body products and more for cleaning, diffusing and room sprays. Pure essential oils can be found at many health food stores, small boutiques, concept stores and online.

I live in the real world and know that, although a very little goes a long way in regard to essential oils, the initial investment with oils such as frankincense and rose is a large one. So, for the purposes of this book and in my own home life, I have kept my list of go-to oils short, versatile and cost effective.

— Bergamot
— Eucalyptus
— Geranium
— Lavender
— Lemon
— Lemongrass
— Orange
— Patchouli
— Peppermint
— Rosemary
— Tea-tree
— Ylang ylang

In many of the recipes you can omit the essential oils altogether or use them interchangeably and as you see fit.

CITRIC ACID
SAL SUDS
WASHING SODA
EPSOM SALTS
ALMOND OIL
EUCALYPTUS AND LEMON SURFACE SPRAY

HONEY

Raw honey has been used since ancient times for a variety of reasons: as a topical ointment for treating wounds and a way to deal with stomach ailments. When it comes to buying honey, it's worth considering quality, potency and ethics. I like to make sure it is raw, from a good source and harvested gently. Look for a trusted honey supplier in your local area and speak to them about their methods. You may also find such people at your local farmer's market or selling online – people who are passionate about growing our dwindling and vital bee population while supporting the health of our environment. Keep in mind that raw honey should never be given to an infant less than a year old.

HYDROGEN PEROXIDE

Nature's simplest peroxide is found in many places, including the human body. It makes for a powerful oxidiser and bleaching agent as well as a very strong antiseptic and, unlike conventional bleach, it's non-toxic. But like many other natural substances, it should be used with caution, and stored correctly. It is unstable and very light-sensitive, so it should be stored in a dark place and ideally in either an amber glass bottle or a completely opaque container. It should also be stored out of the reach of children.

JOJOBA OIL

Jojoba oil makes up approximately 50 per cent of the seeds of the jojoba shrub by weight. It is native to Arizona, California and Mexico, and historically Native Americans used the extracted liquid to treat sores and wounds. The 'oil' derived from the seeds is in fact mostly a wax, accounting for its extreme shelf life and resistance to very high temperatures compared to true vegetable oils. This wonderful topical liquid is a great addition to many natural skincare products, as well as shampoos and conditioners, because it's gentle and non-greasy, and its anti-inflammatory properties help to calm, soothe and moisturise the skin.

OLIVE OIL

Olive oil is produced by pressing whole olives to extract the oil. While commonly used in cooking and in salad dressings, it also makes a wonderful addition to natural skincare and soaps. Olive oil has a long history of being used as a skincare remedy. The ancient Egyptians, Greeks and Romans all used it for cleansing the skin, as a moisturiser and antibacterial agent. Extra virgin, cold-pressed olive oil is my first pick, as it best preserves the oil's quality, and I like to look for varieties that are produced as locally as possible.

PURE LIQUID CASTILE SOAP

Named after the olive oil–based soaps that traditionally come from the Castile region in Spain, this concentrated, natural, non-toxic and biodegradable soap is made from vegetable oils (olive, coconut and hemp, and sometimes oils such as avocado, almond and walnut). It's created in a chemical reaction between the fat (the oil) and a strong alkali called lye in a process called saponification. Some bulk wholefoods stores sell pure liquid castile soap in bulk: just take in your jar and fill it up. I prefer pure (made with 100 per cent organic oils) and unscented so that I can add my preferred essential oils. However, there are some wonderful naturally scented varieties.

ROSE WATER

Rose water is a beautiful and gentle by-product from the production of rose oil. This pure, thin liquid has natural anti-inflammatory properties and has a soft scent that makes it a great addition to many skincare products. Look for organic, 100 per cent rose water with no additives. It is easy to find in health food and wholefoods stores as well as online. I try to buy it in amber glass bottles that help protect it from light. Plus, I can later reuse the bottle to make a nice gift of toner or natural perfume for a friend.

SAL SUDS

Sal suds is a concentrated but mild biodegradable, all-purpose hard-surface cleaner made with plant-based surfactants (compounds that lower the surface tension between two liquids, which acts as a detergent), fir needle and spruce essential oils. It is not a soap, but rather more like a detergent. It is very drying to the skin, so shouldn't be used on the body, but it's a fantastic and effective multi-purpose cleaning product. I buy it from my local bulk wholefoods store, where I take in a container and fill it up at will. You can also find it online and in many other health food and wholefoods stores. A tiny amount goes a very long way in cleaning a surface, making it very cost effective.

SALT

Salt is an ingredient most of us already have on hand. But what kind to use? For cleaning recipes, I use regular old sea salt or table salt. For the food and body recipes, I use a higher quality, mineral-rich salt such as pink salt.

SHEA BUTTER

Shea butter is the fat extracted from the nut of the African shea tree. It melts at body temperature, making it an ideal base for body butters, moisturisers and hair products. It is readily absorbed by the skin. Thick and with a soft feel, a little goes a long way with this very rich ingredient.

SHIKAKAI POWDER

Shikakai powder is dried and ground from the bark, leaves and pods of the shikakai shrub native to the Indian subcontinent. It has been used in Ayurvedic tradition in haircare products for centuries. When developing a natural shampoo recipe, I realised that this was what I was missing: a completely natural, plant-based surfactant that wouldn't be too harsh or drying, would counterbalance the castile soap and help rinse out the product after washing. It is the only ingredient in this book that is used for just the one recipe, but I found it so effective that I had to keep it. So far, I haven't come across it in health food and wholefoods stores, but it can be found online and is well worth tracking down.

SWEET ALMOND OIL

Sweet almond oil is a rich source of vitamin E, which helps to heal and soothe dry skin. It is absorbed relatively quickly and packs a punch of vitamin A as well. It is versatile and easy to come by: just make sure to look for an organic variety. I get mine from my local bulk wholefoods store, but you can also find it online and in many health food stores.

VANILLA OIL

Vanilla oil is sometimes sold as an essential oil, but it actually requires a different type of extraction. The result is not an essential oil at all, but a vanilla-scented oil. Look for organic vanilla CO_2 total extract or *Vanilla plantifolia* extract. Most of the time it will come in a carrier oil such as jojoba. You can also make your own vanilla-scented oil relatively easily. It lends a warm, sweet scent to natural perfumes and essential oil sprays.

VINEGAR (WHITE AND CLEANING)

Vinegar is a non-toxic and very versatile ingredient in many natural DIY recipes. It has been used for thousands of years as an antiseptic. Some people worry that it will make their house smell of vinegar, but the smell evaporates as soon as the surface you are cleaning dries. There are a few things to know about vinegars, though. In their pure, concentrated form, they can be very abrasive to raw materials such as marble, tile grout and untreated wood. Proper dilution is required to avoid staining or degrading such surfaces. It's also important to note that white vinegar and cleaning vinegar are actually two different things. The main difference is that cleaning vinegar has 1 per cent more acidity, making it 20 per cent stronger. Regular white vinegar will still be an effective ingredient for your natural cleaning products, but cleaning vinegar will be more potent and effective. You can find it in supermarkets, bulk wholefoods stores and hardware stores.

VODKA

Vodka is a clear, distilled alcohol that originated in Poland and Russia, traditionally made by distilling fermented liquid from potatoes. Standard vodka contains approximately 40 per cent alcohol. Although traditionally a beverage, I prefer to use it in a few natural cleaning products. Alcohol's quick evaporation helps dry the floor after mopping and to distribute, or 'throw', the beautiful natural scent of essential oils in a room spray. There are varying qualities on the market, so make sure to look for organic, preferably locally made, vodka at your local liquor store.

WASHING SODA (SODA ASH/SODA POWDER)

Washing soda is a water-soluble salt otherwise known as sodium carbonate. It is a slightly alkaline, powerful water softener that helps other cleaning ingredients lift soil from fabrics and suspend soil in wash water. It is cheap and easy to find: some supermarkets sell it. I like to buy mine from my local bulk wholefoods store, and I have also found it packaged at health food stores and grocers. Although it is non-toxic, the powder is very fine, so take care not to breathe it in. I also recommend wearing gloves when handling it as, being a salt, it can irritate some people's skin. Keep in mind that, unlike bicarb soda, washing soda isn't suitable for baking or any skincare products.

WATER

This one's pretty self-explanatory! Just keep in mind that for most of the recipes in this book, filtered water is best. While you don't need to worry too much about it when it comes to something like dog shampoo, filtered is a good idea when it's going to be used on your own skin and hair.

WITCH HAZEL

Witch hazel is a watery liquid derived from a deciduous shrub. It can be used topically as a gentle astringent, making it great in natural and simple DIY body recipes such as skin toner. Make sure to look for an organic variety. You can find it online and in select health food and wholefoods stores.

XYLITOL

Xylitol is a naturally occurring alcohol that you'll find in most plant material. Extracted and turned into a powder, xylitol is widely used as a sugar substitute. Not many people are aware that it is toxic for dogs, so keep it away from your pooch! I use it in my DIY toothpaste recipe to balance out the salty taste of the active ingredient, bicarb soda. You can find xylitol at most health food and wholefoods stores, as well as select bulk food stores and online.

HOME

I used to dread cleaning because of the harsh chemicals, which always gave me a nasty headache. But with these simple natural recipes, now I enjoy it. Although some natural products get a bad rap in terms of their effectiveness, I've found you don't need to use harsh chemicals to get the job done. This chapter contains all the low-cost cleaners I love to make and use, all of which are earth friendly, low tox and free of synthetic fragrances. But it isn't just about cleanliness. The kind of space you create can have a profound effect on your mood, productivity, mental clarity and so much more, which is why I've included a few recipes and rituals to help you create a space that is equally conducive to work and play, productivity and calm. Stored properly, these products should last for a long while, but always use your best judgement. If you're worried, make smaller batches that you'll use more quickly.

TOOLS

- Glass jars
- Glass or recycled plastic spray bottles
- Narrow-mouthed funnel
- Mop
- Broom
- Dustpan
- Natural bin bags
- Cotton cloths and rags, preferably upcycled
- Steel/wooden pegs
- Squeegee
- Small brush or toothbrush
- Bottle brush
- Scrubber brush
- Copper pot scrubber
- Wooden dish scrubber
- Coconut-fibre dish scrubber
- Natural dishwashing gloves
- Diffuser

TIPS FOR FRESHENING YOUR SPACE

- Clear clutter before you start cleaning. Use your intuition and your personality, keeping only items that bring you joy.
- Make sure to ventilate well as you work. Open those windows!
- Add indoor plants to your space to help with air quality.
- Scent the space with essential oils using a diffuser, spray or a beeswax candle. I love the clean, crisp smell of citrus, but there are other options – eucalyptus, rosemary and lavender, to name a few – that will also leave your space smelling clean and fresh. For laundry products, I love using tea-tree, lavender and lemon for their subtle, fresh scents.

MULTI-PURPOSE

MAKES 500 ml (17 fl oz/2 cups)

PREP TIME 2 minutes

EQUIPMENT amber spray bottle + funnel

EUCALYPTUS & LEMON SURFACE SPRAY

I like to keep a bottle of this spray handy on the kitchen counter. Not only does it help to disinfect all kinds of surfaces, but with its bursts of lemon and eucalyptus it also smells so amazingly fresh. It's a great one to use when cleaning up after a meal, and I find it helps eliminate cooking odours.

I use this spray on our stainless-steel benchtops as well as other surfaces. For raw surfaces I use my All-purpose cleaner (page 41), as lemon juice and vinegar are a bit too harsh for things like uncoated timber, tile grout and natural stone. You might also try tea-tree, rosemary, sweet orange, peppermint or lavender essential oils in this recipe for a fresh, clean, calming space.

250 ml (8½ fl oz/1 cup) filtered water

240 ml (8 fl oz) cleaning vinegar

juice of 1 lemon, strained

20 drops lemon essential oil

10 drops eucalyptus essential oil

Combine all ingredients in the spray bottle. Attach the lid and give it a shake. Store in a cool, dark place.

TO USE Spray over the surface to be cleaned and wipe it with a clean cloth.

EUCALYPTUS
AND
LEMON
SURFACE
SPRAY

ALL
PURPOSE

MAKES 500 ml (17 fl oz/2 cups)

PREP TIME 2 minutes

EQUIPMENT amber spray bottle + funnel

ALL-PURPOSE CLEANER

A little definitely goes a very long way when it comes to this cleaner. You may be surprised just how little you need to move stubborn dirt. Vinegar can be too dehydrating and abrasive on some raw surfaces such as wood and natural stone, making this version of an all-purpose cleaner a much gentler option for more delicate surfaces that are still in need of a clean. It is also super economical! The active ingredient, sal suds, is a biodegradable concentrated hard surface cleaner made of naturally derived plant surfactants (page 27). I love adding some extra lemon essential oil to this one for a delicious fresh scent, but it is totally optional.

500 ml (17 fl oz/2 cups) filtered water

2 teaspoons sal suds

20 drops lemon essential oil (optional)

Combine all ingredients in the spray bottle. Attach the lid and give it a good shake.

TO USE Spray over the surface to be cleaned and wipe it with a clean cloth. If dirt is proving particularly stubborn, spray and leave it for a few minutes before scrubbing.

GLASS CLEANER

MAKES 500 ml (17 fl oz/2 cups)

PREP TIME 2 minutes

EQUIPMENT amber spray bottle + funnel

Who would have thought that vinegar, water and essential oils are all you need for sparklingly clean windows? It's oh-so simple, tox free, all natural and made from ingredients you may already have on hand! My favourite essential oils to use here are citrus for their fresh and clean scent. Eucalyptus and rosemary also make great additions. The vodka is there purely to aid the evaporation process, and I find it works really well. If you'd like to omit it, though, the recipe will still be effective.

375 ml (12½/1½ cups) filtered water

60 ml (2 fl oz/¼ cup) organic vodka

60 ml (2 fl oz/¼ cup) cleaning vinegar

20 drops lemon essential oil

10 drops eucalyptus essential oil

Combine all ingredients in the spray bottle. Attach the lid and shake well. Store in a cool, dark place.

TO USE Shake well. Spray over the window surface and polish with a microfibre cloth or recycled paper towel. If your glass is particularly dirty, use the All-purpose cleaner (page 41) beforehand.

FLOOR
CLEANER

MAKES 500 ml (17 fl oz/2 cups)

PREP TIME 2 minutes

EQUIPMENT amber glass bottle + funnel

FLOOR CLEANER

Let's be honest: mopping the floor is a mundane job and most of us would prefer that we didn't have to do it. I still don't jump at the chance, but at least with this recipe on hand I no longer mind it. It's actually a good opportunity to make your space smell clean and fresh. I like to use citrus or eucalyptus oils to leave the house smelling amazing. The vodka will help the floor dry more quickly. I also like to use hot water to make it dry even faster, mainly because of my dog, Fred. He's good at opening the door right after I've mopped and traipsing dirt straight over, so the faster my floor dries the better!

250 ml (8½ fl oz/1 cup) cleaning vinegar

150 ml (5 fl oz) filtered water

60 ml (2 fl oz/¼ cup) organic vodka

2 tablespoons sal suds

1 teaspoon jojoba oil

30 drops eucalyptus essential oil

10 drops orange essential oil

Combine all ingredients in the bottle. Attach the lid and shake well. Store in a cool, dark place.

TO USE Shake well and add approximately 2 tablespoons to a bucket of hot water and mop the floor as normal. For uncoated wooden floors, use the Wood surface cleaner (page 46) instead.

MAKES 500 ml (17 fl oz/2 cups)

PREP TIME 2 minutes

EQUIPMENT amber spray bottle + funnel

WOOD SURFACE CLEANER

If your uncoated timber surfaces are looking a little dull, try using this surface cleaner to refresh them. It cleans them gently and leaves them with a beautiful, subtle shine. All you need is a clean cloth or rag and some elbow grease. It works perfectly on finely sanded surfaces and ones buffed with natural oil, such as timber flooring and furniture, and I love the beautiful orange scent it leaves behind. Just make sure to shake the mixture well before using, as oil, water and vinegar tend to separate.

125 ml (4 fl oz/½ cup) almond or olive oil

65 ml (2¼ fl oz/¼ cup) cleaning vinegar

310 ml (10½ fl oz/1¼ cups) filtered water

25 drops orange essential oil, or your oil of choice

Combine the oil and vinegar in your spray bottle. Top with filtered water and your essential oil of choice. Attach the lid and shake well. Store in a cool, dark place.

TO USE Shake well. Spray onto the wood surface, then wipe it with a clean cloth or rag, always moving in the direction of the wood grain. To clean small areas, spray the mixture directly onto the cloth. After cleaning, you can buff the wood with a dry cloth for a more polished finish.

WOOD
CLEANER

LOVE
TEA

RUST REMOVER

MAKES 1.25 litres (42 fl oz/5 cups)

PREP TIME 2 minutes

STEEP TIME 2–4 hours

EQUIPMENT large pot or saucepan

I use this recipe to remove rust from utensils, gardening tools (such as secateurs) and other small items. I find it particularly handy for cleaning rusty items bought second hand. It's pretty crazy what the tannic acid in plain old black tea can do to renew these well-used items! It's a simple process, and way more economical (and less wasteful) than throwing them out.

about 1.25 litres (42 fl oz/5 cups) filtered water

3 black tea bags

In a large saucepan, bring the water to boil. Turn off the heat, add the teabags and let them steep until the water's cooled, about 20–30 minutes. Add in any rusty items you want to clean, removing the tea bags first if you wish. Allow them to soak for a few hours, then rinse clean. Double or triple the recipe and the size of the pot to accommodate the size of your rusty items. It's best used fresh.

CREAM CLEANSER

MAKES about 230 g (8 oz/¾ cup)

PREP TIME 2 minutes

EQUIPMENT medium bowl, mixing spoon + airtight jar

For stubborn grime, grease and rust stains, I find this cream cleanser really does the trick. Its gentle scouring power will lift any dirt and grime with ease. The gentle abrasion from the bicarb soda combined with castile soap makes for an effective heavy-duty cleaner. I use it in the shower on soap scum and to lift rust from our stainless-steel benchtops. The essential oils are totally optional, but I think they contribute to its power.

180 g (6½ oz/1 cup) bicarbonate of soda (baking soda)

20 drops lemon essential oil

10 drops eucalyptus essential oil

2 drops tea-tree essential oil

3 tablespoons pure liquid castile soap, plus more if needed

In a bowl, combine the bicarb soda and essential oils. While stirring, slowly pour in the castile soap and mix until it becomes a smooth paste. Transfer to a small airtight jar or similar container to store. It can dry out over long periods: if that happens, add more castile soap and mix.

TO USE Add a teaspoon or more to a clean cloth. Run cream over the surface to be cleaned, lightly scrubbing until any dirt and grime comes away. Rinse or wipe the surface clean.

BAKING
SODA
CASTILE
SOAP
CREAM
CLEANSER

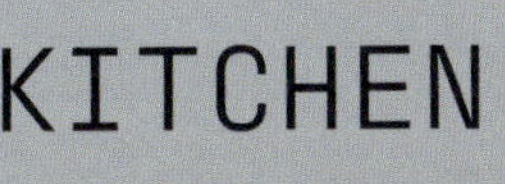

KITCHEN

MAKES 1 tablespoon

PREP TIME 1 minute

EQUIPMENT small bowl + mixing spoon

METAL UTENSIL, SAUCEPAN & TRAY CLEANER

This simple cleaner works in the same way as my oven cleaner to refresh tired old pans, baking trays and cooking utensils. This recipe makes enough to cover the entire inside of a large saucepan. You can use the same ratio of bicarb soda and water to make more or less depending on what you are cleaning.

2 tablespoons bicarbonate of soda (baking soda)

1 tablespoon filtered water

In a small bowl, combine the bicarb soda and water to form a thick paste.

TO USE Spread the paste across the inside of saucepans and oven trays, as well as over metal utensils and plastic chopping boards. Let it sit for 30 minutes or more (overnight works well). Scrub clean with a gentle scourer and rinse with warm water.

SCONE TRAY

TABLESPOON

MAKES enough to clean 1 chopping board

PREP TIME 2 minutes

EQUIPMENT none

WOODEN CHOPPING BOARD CLEANER & STAIN REMOVER

Herbs, fruits and veggies often leave chopping boards with stains. Cleaning them periodically with this super-simple mixture helps lift them out, and it's a great way to give your boards a good clean and refresh. This recipe makes enough to cover the surface of an average-size wooden chopping board, but you can use this ratio of salt to lemon to make more or less depending on how many you're cleaning. It works best when done straight after food preparation.

1 tablespoon coarse salt

half a lemon

TO USE Sprinkle the salt over the surface of the chopping board. Squeeze the lemon over, then scrub the wood to lift out stains. Rinse well and stand upright to dry.

MAKES 500 ml (17 fl oz/2 cups)

PREP TIME 2 minutes

EQUIPMENT amber pump bottle + funnel

DISH LIQUID

This natural dish liquid is just as effective as all the store-bought versions I've used in the past. I love that, with some basic ingredients, I can quickly whip up a new batch whenever we run out. If you do a lot of dishes, you may like to invest in some quality natural rubber gloves as they really do save your hands from drying out. I find that lemon essential oil lends it a deliciously fresh scent, but there are many other oils that make a nice addition. Try orange, rosemary, lavender and eucalyptus.

375 ml (12½ fl oz/1½ cups) filtered water

50 ml (1¾ fl oz/¼ cup) cleaning vinegar

1 tablespoon jojoba or sweet almond oil

30 drops lemon essential oil

60 ml (2 fl oz/¼ cup) sal suds

Combine all ingredients in your pump bottle, adding the sal suds last.

TO USE Shake a few times. Hand wash your dishes as normal.

DISH
LIQUID

BAKING
SODA

DISHWASHING TABLETS

MAKES about 24 small tablets

PREP TIME 5 minutes

EQUIPMENT natural rubber gloves, large bowl, mixing spoon, 2 ice cube trays (silicone if you have them) + lidded jar

These tablets are a great, easy way to avoid using chemicals without compromising on effectiveness. I like to make a few batches at a time so that we are nice and stocked up.

- 240 g (8½ oz/1 cup) washing soda
- 120 g (4½ oz/½ cup) Epsom salts
- 90 g (3 oz/½ cup) bicarbonate of soda (baking soda)
- 20 drops lemon essential oil (optional)
- 80 ml (2½ fl oz/⅓ cup) fresh lemon juice

Pull on gloves to protect your hands from the washing soda. In a large bowl, combine the washing soda, Epsom salts, bicarb soda and essential oil if using. Slowly add in the lemon juice, mixing as you pour. It will fizz as the lemon juice and bicarb react with each other. Continue to stir until well combined. Spoon the mixture into the ice cube trays and firmly press each one down. Set aside to dry for about 24 hours. Once set, pop the tablets out of the trays and store them in a lidded jar or container.

TO USE Just use them as you would a store-bought dishwasher tablet. If you normally use a rinse aid, I find that 2 tablespoons of white vinegar added to the rinse-aid compartment does the trick.

MAKES 610 g (1 lb 6 oz)

PREP TIME 2 minutes

EQUIPMENT natural rubber gloves, a large bowl, spoon + airtight container

DISHWASHING POWDER

Store-bought dishwashing powders and tablets contain strong, harsh chemicals. Why not use a gentler, more natural version that you can feel good about? If you have a particularly dirty load, you may want to rinse the contents first to give this gentle cleaner the best chance possible.

240 g (8½ oz/1 cup) washing soda

180 g (6½ oz/1 cup) bicarbonate of soda (baking soda)

130 g (4½ oz/½ cup) salt

60 g (2 oz/¼ cup) citric acid

25 drops lemon or orange essential oil

Pull on gloves to protect your hands from the washing soda. In a large bowl, combine all ingredients and mix well to combine. Transfer the powder to an airtight container. You may want to include a measuring spoon for ease of use.

TO USE Make sure your dishwasher is clean before using this powder for the first time. Pour 1 tablespoon of the powder into the tablet or powder compartment of your dishwasher, and wash as normal. If you normally use a rinse aid, I find that 2 tablespoons of white vinegar added to the rinse-aid compartment works well.

TABLESPOON

STOVETOP CLEANER

MAKES enough for 1 clean

PREP TIME 2 minutes

DEVELOPMENT TIME 20 minutes

EQUIPMENT none

I have found this super-simple cleaner effective for removing absolutely everything from the surface of my stove, and with very little effort. No harsh chemicals required! It smells deliciously fresh, thanks to the lemon and the deodorising magic of the bicarb soda. Is there anything bicarb and fresh lemon can't do?

3 tablespoons bicarbonate of soda (baking soda)

1 fresh lemon

Sprinkle the bicarb soda all over your stovetop. Cut the lemon in half and squeeze the juice over the bicarb soda. It will bubble and fizz a little as the two react. Take the squeezed lemon halves and rub them over the surface of your stovetop.

TO USE Leave it for up to 20 minutes so the mixture can work its magic, then wipe clean.

For a super-sparkling finish, follow it up with the Glass cleaner (page 42) to remove any traces of bicarb soda.

OVEN CLEANER

MAKES 145 g (4½ oz/½ cup)

PREP TIME 2 minutes

DEVELOPMENT TIME 30 minutes

EQUIPMENT small bowl + spoon

This method of cleaning the inside and glass of your oven is so simple, and it requires very little elbow grease to boot. The main ingredient here is time, and you don't even need that much of it! The bicarb works to loosen baked-on grease and grime. Once it has worked its magic, a gentle scrub with a cloth finishes the job. Water, bicarb and essential oils: it doesn't get much more natural than that. The quantities in this recipe are a rough estimate to make enough to clean an average-size oven. You can adjust the quantities to suit your needs.

90 g (3 oz/½ cup) bicarbonate of soda (baking soda)

60 ml (2 fl oz/¼ cup) filtered water

5 drops lemon or orange essential oil

In a small bowl, combine the bicarb soda, water and essential oil and stir to form a thick paste.

TO USE Spread the paste over the dirty areas of your oven and leave it to sit for 30 minutes or more. You might even leave it overnight. Wipe clean with a wet dish cloth or recycled paper towel. For a sparkling finish, follow it up with the Glass cleaner (page 42).

HAND
SOAP
TOOTH
PASTE

BATHROOM

MAKES 500 ml (17 fl oz/2 cups)

PREP TIME 2 minutes

EQUIPMENT amber spray bottle + funnel

BATHROOM CLEANER

In the world of home cleaners, the words 'no-scrub' and 'natural' don't often coexist, especially with bathroom and shower cleaners. But this one is the exception. The powerful combination of sal suds and white cleaning vinegar work together to do most of the cleaning for you, making it effective without a lot of effort. Your reward is a sparkling clean bathroom ready to light some candles, run a hot bath and relax, satisfied that you have created a clean space without using harsh chemicals. Especially satisfying on shower glass! If you don't have lemon or tea-tree essential oils on hand, I also love orange, grapefruit, eucalyptus, lavender and lemongrass. After cleaning our shower I love to add a sprig of eucalyptus, either in a vase or hung from the shower head, for an extra burst of freshness.

250 ml (8½ fl oz/1 cup) cleaning vinegar

125 ml (4 fl oz/½ cup) sal suds

125 ml (4 fl oz/½ cup) filtered water

15 drops lemon essential oil

3 drops tea-tree essential oil

Combine all ingredients in the spray bottle. Attach the lid and shake to combine.

TO USE Spray over the surface to be cleaned. Wipe the spray with a cloth before rinsing it with water to remove both the product and dirt. For more stubborn grime, you may need to use a little elbow grease along with a scrubbing brush. Remember that vinegar can damage some natural, uncoated surfaces. For these, use the All-purpose cleaner (page 41) or Wood surface cleaner (page 46).

BATH
ROOM
CLEANER

TOILET BOWL CLEANER

MAKES 500 ml (17 fl oz/2 cups)

PREP TIME 2 minutes

EQUIPMENT spray bottle, funnel + icing sugar shaker

Sometimes the good old-fashioned cleaning method is the best one – regular old cleaning vinegar and bicarb soda. When combined, they react to make a powerful and natural cleaning force. Bicarb is a wonderful mild abrasive, gentle enough for enamelware in bathrooms and many other surfaces. I like to store mine in a labelled icing-sugar shaker in the cleaning cupboard, as it makes shaking it out onto a surface that much easier.

375 ml (12½ fl oz/1½ cups) filtered water

125 ml (4 fl oz/½ cup) cleaning vinegar

180 g (6½ oz/1 cup) bicarbonate of soda (baking soda)

Combine the water and vinegar in your spray bottle. Attach the lid and shake to combine. If you don't have it on hand already, fill the icing shaker with the bicarb soda.

TO USE Spray the inside of the toilet bowl with the vinegar and water mixture, covering as much of the surface as possible, then shake the bicarb soda over the top. The vinegar and bicarb will fizz a little. Use a natural toilet brush, such as one made with coconut fibre, to scrub the inside of the toilet bowl before flushing. To clean the rest of the toilet, such as the outer cistern and seat, the Bathroom cleaner (page 70) and All-purpose cleaner (page 41) work really well.

MAKES about 200 ml (7 fl oz) of spray

PREP TIME 2 minutes

EQUIPMENT funnel, 2 spray bottles + icing sugar shaker

BLEACH-FREE MOULD REMOVER

That pesky mould! It manages to find its way into any damp areas, especially if they aren't well ventilated. I like to open the windows in our bathroom at least once a day to let the fresh air in. Of course, that can be difficult to do in some bathrooms, and in some weather. When it does creep in, we can combat it using the power of simple, natural ingredients such as cleaning vinegar, tea-tree oil (a powerful disinfectant) and bicarb soda. This recipe has two parts: the first helps you stop mould in its tracks, while the second (optional) part prevents it from returning. A powerful one-two punch!

200 ml (7 fl oz) cleaning vinegar

20 drops tea-tree oil (you could also try eucalyptus, lemon or lavender)

180 g (6½ oz/1 cup) bicarbonate of soda (baking soda)

100 ml (3½ fl oz) hydrogen peroxide (optional)

Pour the vinegar and tea-tree oil into a 200 ml (7 fl oz) spray bottle and shake well. Add the bicarb soda to the shaker.

TO USE Spray the vinegar over any mouldy surfaces. Shake the bicarb over the top and leave it to air dry. Lightly scrub with a cloth, then wipe away and rinse clean.

To prevent mould from returning, fill a 100 ml (3½ fl oz) spray bottle with hydrogen peroxide and spray a very small amount over the surface after cleaning, leaving it to dry completely. If you have any super-stubborn mould or mildew, you might like to try the Cream cleanser (page 50) first.

CREAM
CLEANSER
HYDROGEN
PEROXIDE
BAKING
SODA

FRESH
AIR
CLEAN & SMOOTH
This is a great value vodka that is perfect for cocktails and parties.
VODKA
5 TIMES DISTILLED
700mL
37.0% ALC/VOL

MAKES about 200 ml (7 fl oz)

PREP TIME 2 minutes

EQUIPMENT amber spray bottle + funnel

FRESH AIR BATHROOM SPRAY

A fresh-smelling bathroom is easy to achieve with a few natural ingredients and a spray bottle. The vodka helps distribute the beautiful natural scents of the essential oils, but if you would prefer to leave it out, you absolutely can. Play around with your favourite essential oils in this one. I like to use orange, rosemary, peppermint, lavender, grapefruit and lime.

40 drops lemon essential oil

20 drops eucalyptus essential oil

5 drops lemongrass essential oil

160 ml (5½ fl oz/⅔ cup) filtered water

2 tablespoons organic vodka

Add the essential oils to your spray bottle, then pour in the water and vodka. Shake before each use.

TO USE Spray a few times into the air, upwards and away from your face.

LAUNDRY

MAKES about 1 litre (34 fl oz/4 cups)

PREP TIME 10 minutes

EQUIPMENT medium saucepan, natural rubber gloves, whisk, spoon, funnel + large jar or bottle

LAUNDRY LIQUID

Laundry detergents can contain all sorts of nasty chemicals, polluting our environment and leaving residue on clothes that you then wear against your skin. Not to mention the overpowering synthetic fragrances! These simple ingredients do a beautiful job of cleaning our clothes, which is no mean feat after a big gardening session or a trip away with mountain bikes, surf boards and hiking gear in tow. Try playing around with the essential oils in this recipe to create your favourite scent. Some of my favourite combinations for laundry liquid are lemon + tea-tree, orange + eucalyptus and tea-tree + lavender. For this version I have used geranium + eucalyptus for a fresh and floral scent.

1 litre (34 fl oz/4 cups) filtered water

160 g (5½ oz/⅔ cup) washing soda

45 g (1½ oz/¼ cup) bicarbonate of soda (baking soda)

125 ml (4 fl oz/½ cup) sal suds

10 drops eucalyptus essential oil

2 drops geranium essential oil

Pour the water into a saucepan and bring it to the boil. Pull on rubber gloves to protect your hands from the washing soda. Turn the heat off, then add the washing and bicarb sodas. Whisk until dissolved. Add the sal suds and stir well. Add the essential oils and stir again. Once the mixture has cooled to room temperature, use a funnel to transfer it to a bottle or jar.

TO USE Shake the mixture a few times before each use, as the bicarb soda can settle at the bottom. Use 40–60 ml (1¼–2 fl oz) per load of washing, depending on your machine and the size of the load. Where we live it gets fairly chilly over winter, and I have found that this mixture can solidify a little after a few cold nights. All I do is add a little water and shake until it is liquid again.

LAUNDRY
LIQUID

EPSOM
SALTS
CITRIC
ACID
SEA SALT
WASHING
SODA
BAKING
SODA

MAKES 675 g (1½ lb/2½ cups)

PREP TIME 2 minutes

EQUIPMENT natural rubber gloves + large, lidded glass jar

LAUNDRY POWDER

This recipe is beautifully simple to make and use, not to mention economical! It is well worth the small amount of effort it takes to make a batch every now and then. Plus, I think a jar of any shape and size beats a brightly coloured branded box or thick plastic bottle on the laundry shelf. Don't you agree?

250 g (9 oz/1 cup) washing soda

150 g (5½ oz/½ cup) salt

125 g (4½ oz/½ cup) citric acid

90 g (3 oz/½ cup) bicarbonate of soda (baking soda)

60 g (2 oz/¼ cup) Epsom salts

20 drops tea-tree essential oil

20 drops lavender essential oil

Pull on gloves to protect your hands from the washing soda. Add all ingredients to a large glass jar, close the lid and shake really well to combine.

TO USE Use 2 tablespoons per average load of washing.

MAKES about 350 ml (12 fl oz)

PREP TIME 2 minutes

EQUIPMENT medium bowl, mixing spoon + airtight amber glass jar

NATURAL CLOTHES WHITENER & STAIN REMOVER

Over time, our white clothing tends to discolour a little. It can be tempting to use a harsh store-bought bleach to bring it back to a vibrant white, but what if there was a more natural alternative? Here we have it: a simple, all-natural recipe to restore your whites. I have used it on my white shirts countless times now, and each time I am amazed at the results. The other fabulous benefit is that the concentrate doubles as a natural and effective stain remover.

160 g (5½ oz/⅔ cup) lemon juice

30 drops lemon essential oil

60 ml (2 fl oz/¼ cup) hydrogen peroxide

180 g (6½ oz/1 cup) bicarbonate of soda (baking soda)

In a bowl, combine the lemon juice, essential oil and hydrogen peroxide. Add the bicarb soda very slowly, stirring constantly. It will react with the other ingredients and fizz a little. Once it is all combined, pour it into an airtight amber glass jar (to protect the potency of the active ingredients) and store in a cool, dry place. Shake well before each use.

TO USE AS A WHITENER Fill a bucket or sink with warm water. Add 2 tablespoons for every garment you are soaking and stir well. Add your garments and mix a few times, making sure they are fully submerged. Leave to soak for 12 hours or overnight, then wash as normal and air dry. The sun is a fabulous disinfectant!

To restore brightness to white laundry more regularly, add a teaspoon or so to your washing load along with the natural Laundry liquid (page 80).

TO USE AS A STAIN REMOVER Gently rub a small amount into any stained area(s) with a small brush. Leave it to sit for about 2 hours before washing.

MAKES 140 ml (4½ fl oz)

PREP TIME 2 minutes

EQUIPMENT jar or bottle

FRED'S WASH (DOG SHAMPOO)

Fred really dislikes being washed. Fortunately for us, we live close to the beach and he gets a good rinse most days. When we do give him a little freshen up, this is the recipe we use. The lavender essential oil is there for a subtle, calming scent that, incidentally, fleas do not like! It is important to note that some essential oils are toxic to dogs, so if you wish to use a different oil for smell it is super important to do your research or consult your vet. The castile soap foams and cleans nicely, while the olive oil nourishes and moisturises. The apple-cider vinegar is naturally antibacterial, works to eliminate odours, and helps to condition and bring shine to his coat while helping to remove any residue. This quantity is enough for one wash with Fred, who is medium sized, so just adjust the amount depending on your dog.

- 3 tablespoons pure liquid castile soap
- 2 tablespoons filtered water
- 1½ tablespoons apple-cider vinegar
- 3 teaspoons olive oil
- 2 drops lavender essential oil

Combine all ingredients in a jar or bottle and shake really well to combine.

TO USE Wet your pooch with warm water. Lather the shampoo into your dog's fur, avoiding their face and eyes. Rinse thoroughly.

FLEETWOOD MAC

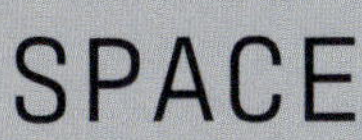

SPACE

MAKES 100 ml (3½ fl oz)

PREP TIME 2 minutes

EQUIPMENT funnel + amber spray bottle

ROOM SPRAY, THREE WAYS

I live in a very small space, so I find opening the windows to let fresh air in important. Adding some beautiful scents as well really helps to create a nice atmosphere. These beautifully scented mists are a staple in our house. Here are three favourite combinations I like to have on hand for different purposes and times of day. In flow lives on the bench in our living room (I love to use it to lightly scent the room before guests arrive), Swell resides in our bed nook to spray when settling in for a good night's rest and Bush walk sits on my desk, where it helps refresh and clear the room before I start work. You could also try these essential oil combinations in your diffuser, if you have one.

IN FLOW

(elevate ~ happiness ~ contentment)

25 drops orange

5 drops ylang ylang

5 drops vanilla oil

1 drop geranium

SWELL

(calm ~ soothe ~ relax)

20 drops lavender

5 drops patchouli

5 drops vanilla oil

BUSH WALK

(freshen ~ clear ~ think)

20 drops lemon

5 drops bergamot

2 drops peppermint

2 drops eucalyptus

1 drop rosemary

30–40 drops essential oils (see above)

1 tablespoon witch hazel

1 tablespoon organic vodka

60 ml (2 fl oz/¼ cup) filtered water

Combine all ingredients in a spray bottle and shake well to combine.

TO USE Shake well before each use and spray into the air, slightly upwards and away from your face.

IN
FLOW
SWELL
BUSH
WALK

MAKES 2 sticks

PREP TIME 5 minutes

EQUIPMENT scissors

HERB BUNDLE

The smoke of a herb bundle is said to help purify the air, clear negative energy and bring good vibes into a space. It is best done after cleaning, which is why I have included this simple recipe. I believe in ritual and respecting your space, and I enjoy this practice after a good spring clean. It's also a great way to use up leftover herbs from the garden. As an added bonus, these pretty little bundles of good vibes make sweet and thoughtful gifts.

20 g (2–4 stalks) fresh sage stalks

20 g (2–4 stalks) fresh rosemary stalks

20 g (2–4 stalks) fresh lavender stalks

4 metres (13 ft) natural twine such as cotton, jute or hemp, cut into two equal lengths

Divide the herbs and lavender into two bunches. Strip the very bottom of the stalks (about 3 cm/1¼ in up from the ends) of any leaves. Take one piece of twine and tie one end around the base of a bunch. Wind it tightly all the way around to the top of the bunch and back down again, repeating until you use the whole length of twine. Tie it tightly around the base of the bunch again, knotting it to keep it from unravelling. Trim the stalks down to just above the top of the twine on both ends.

Repeat these steps to form your second herb bundle. Hang them both upside-down for approximately 2 weeks to dry.

TO USE Open all of your windows. Light the very top of your herb bundle, then immediately blow out the flame. The end will be smoking. Angle the herb bundle upward and set a positive intention for your space. Productivity, clarity, calm, acceptance: you name it. Keeping that intention in mind, move slowly through the room, especially into the corners. Once you are done, place the end of the stick under running water, then in a heatproof bowl to dry. Once dry, you can use it again.

MAKES 2 × 250 ml (8½ fl oz/1 cup) candles (about 30 hours of burn time)

PREP TIME 20 minutes

EQUIPMENT clean glass or ceramic cups (about 7 cm/2¾ in both height and diameter), chopsticks or skewers, 2 braided cotton wicks, medium saucepan, large wide-mouth glass jar + scissors

BEESWAX CANDLES

I started making my own beeswax candles to make use of some old jars and ceramic vessels. Store-bought beeswax candles can be expensive, making this DIY project a smart one if you are after a cleaner, greener candle. Beeswax has a much higher melting point than other waxes used in candle making, which means the candle burns slower and for longer. Because it requires little to no chemical processing, it is a pure, clean wax that will not omit any nasties. In fact, it will help purify your home.

300 g (10½ oz) beeswax pastilles, or grated beeswax (for a vegan option, use 150 g/5½ oz candelilla wax)

125 ml (4 fl oz/½ cup) coconut oil

about 80 drops of your essential oil blend of choice (try the combinations on page 90)

5 drops vanilla oil (optional)

Place a chopstick or skewer across the top and in the centre of each vessel and gently wind the top of the wick around it. Make sure the base of the wick is touching the base of the vessel.

Half-fill a saucepan with water and warm it over a low heat. Add the beeswax pastilles and coconut oil to a wide-mouth glass jar (I have a designated one I use for candle making, as beeswax is not the easiest thing to clean off). Stand it in the water. Once the oil and beeswax turn liquid, add the essential oils and vanilla oil and stir well.

Carefully divide the mixture between the two vessels, making sure each wick remains upright and centred. Leave them to cool for about 30 minutes. Trim the wick to 1 cm (½ in).

TO USE Allow 2–4 hours of burn time for the first burn before blowing it out to ensure it doesn't 'funnel' in the centre.

MAKES 1 bunch

PREP TIME 20 minutes

EQUIPMENT twine + scissors

AIR-DRIED FLOWERS

Over the past few years I have really enjoyed growing and selecting beautiful Australian natives and other flowers and foliage to air dry, using them to decorate our space with everlasting beauty! If we have a surplus of our favourites growing in the garden, I can make their natural beauty last for many seasons with zero maintenance required.

1 fistful of fresh flowers from the garden

Select your flowers. Small, sturdy flowers work best: think strawflowers (pictured), also called paper daisies, baby's breath, lavender, globe thistle, cornflower and statice. Most flowers air dry best when they are just beginning to open.

Strip each flower of its leaves. Collect them in bunches of up to eight stems. Very large flowers such as proteas should be hung individually or in a bunch of just two. Tie each bunch together with twine, just a couple of centimetres from the end. Hang them upside down in a cool, dry place out of direct sunlight for 4 weeks or more.

Once they're dry, I like to arrange them in a vase or use them in gift wrapping. Be gentle, though; dried flowers are delicate.

MAKES 1 fly trap

PREP TIME 2 minutes

EQUIPMENT jar, mixing spoon, 1 A4 sheet of paper + tape

FLY TRAP

One thing we are adamant about in our house is composting our veggie scraps. Before they make their way out to our worm farm or compost system, they are added to a small container on the kitchen bench. This container tends to attract teeny tiny flies, so I just set this fly trap next to it: problem solved. I have also found this simple contraption does the trick when it comes to larger flies. I love that I can just set it and forget it, confident that I am not polluting the air we breathe with nasty chemicals from more conventional fly and bug sprays. Plus, it's made from just a few basic items you may already have on hand.

100 ml (3½ fl oz) water

2 tablespoons apple-cider vinegar

1 tablespoon honey or maple syrup

1 teaspoon sal suds

In your jar, combine all ingredients and stir well. Roll the paper into a cone shape and tape to secure it. Place your makeshift funnel in the jar, narrow end down, making sure to leave at least 2 cm (¾ in) between paper and liquid.

TO USE Put in an open area out of the reach of children. I've left mine out for up to 1 month.

BODY

Learning that much of what we put onto our skin is absorbed straight into our bloodstream made me very aware of what I was putting on my body. Luckily, there are plenty of naturally occurring and minimally processed plant oils and gels, vinegars, waxes and pure plant extracts that are more than effective in personal care products. These can be soothing, cleansing, deeply moisturising and nourishing, not to mention easy to prepare, long-lasting and cost effective. So why are there such complicated, long lists of ingredients in conventional products? In this chapter you will discover my super-simple recipes for the body care products I make at home. Using these has saved me time and money, and they've also empowered me to better look after myself.

TOOLS

- Assorted jars and spray bottles
- Upcycled makeup pots
- Immersion blender/food processor
- Double boiler (you can also make one by placing a heatproof bowl over a saucepan)
- Assorted saucepans and a kettle
- Silicone cupcake trays
- Whisk
- Mixing spoons
- Safety razor
- Hemp exfoliating washcloth (page 151)
- Face cloth/washer
- Dry body brush
- Bamboo toothbrush
- Washable cotton makeup remover pads
- Wooden hairbrush
- Comb

TOOTH
PASTE

MAKES about 170 g (6 oz/½ cup)

PREP TIME 10 minutes

EQUIPMENT food processor, double boiler, mixing spoon + airtight jar with lid

TOOTHPASTE

I find it so satisfying to make my own super-simple toothpaste at home, from scratch and with ingredients from my pantry. All are inexpensive and easy to find at your local bulk wholefoods store. You'll not only avoid packaging waste, you'll upcycle a small jar or container as well. This recipe can take some getting used to, as the active ingredient – bicarb soda – can taste a bit salty. If you are after a sweeter version, simply add more xylitol and peppermint essential oil. I love it and I hope you do too!

50 g (1¾ oz/¼ cup) xylitol

60 ml (2 fl oz/¼ cup) coconut oil

100 g (3½ oz/½ cup) bicarbonate of soda (baking soda)

20–40 drops food-grade organic peppermint essential oil

Blend the xylitol in a food processor until a powder forms. As you remove the lid, be careful not to breathe in the small particles.

In a double boiler, gently melt the coconut oil over a low heat. Add the bicarb soda and xylitol and stir until well combined. Remove from the heat and add the peppermint oil. Stir again and transfer it to a clean glass jar. Once the mixture has cooled to room temperature, attach the jar's lid. Store in a cool, dry place.

TO USE Put approximately ¼ teaspoon onto your toothbrush and brush as normal. You may like to keep a spoon or small wooden spatula with the jar. It makes it easy to scoop out!

MAKES about 100 ml (3½ fl oz), or 5 × 20 ml (¼–¾ fl oz) bars

PREP TIME 5 minutes

EQUIPMENT double boiler, whisk + silicone cupcake tray

DEODORANT BARS

There are great natural deodorant bars on the market these days, but it's satisfying to avoid plastic waste and make your own from scratch, especially when it's this easy and economical! I make a few at a time, and they last for ages. You can store the excess bars in the fridge or give them away as gifts. I love adding tea-tree oil for its antibacterial, anti-fungal and deodorising properties, and lavender for its calming scent. If you live in a hot climate you can repurpose small containers and pour your deodorant into them instead, as the bars will melt at the same rate as chocolate. I live in a cool, dry climate, so find the bar version convenient. I repurpose small calico jewellery bags to store mine in, which works a treat.

100 g (3½ oz) cacao butter, grated or finely chopped

3 tablespoons bicarbonate of soda (baking soda)

2 tablespoons arrowroot powder

10 drops lavender essential oil

2 drops tea-tree essential oil

In a double boiler, gently melt the cacao butter over a low heat. Add in all other ingredients and whisk them well, then pour the mixture into the cupcake tray (for bars) or small containers. Transfer them to the refrigerator for a minimum of 1 hour to set. When they're ready, pop the bars out of the tray and store them in a cool, dry place.

TO USE Apply the same way you would a deodorant stick.

BODY
WASH
OLIVE
OIL

MAKES 375 ml (12½ fl oz/1½ cups)

PREP TIME 2 minutes

EQUIPMENT funnel + foaming pump bottle

MOISTURISING BODY WASH

This deeply nourishing body wash feels so luxurious on your skin. The combination of honey and olive oil helps moisturise your skin while the castile soap cleanses it. I like to add fresh, light-smelling essential oils and mix it up with each batch I make. Some of my favourites are eucalyptus, tea-tree, orange, lemon, lime, peppermint and grapefruit. If you are after more soothing and floral scents, geranium and lavender work a treat. The beauty of this recipe is that you only need a little for a good lather, which means you get good bang for your buck! Storing it in a foaming bottle will make it stretch even further. I like to use it with the Hemp exfoliating wash cloth (page 151) to exfoliate, moisturise, nourish and clean all at the same time.

125 ml (4 fl oz/½ cup) pure liquid castile soap

125 ml (4 fl oz/½ cup) filtered water

60 ml (2 fl oz/¼ cup) organic cold-pressed olive oil

60 ml (2 fl oz/¼ cup) local honey (or olive, jojoba or sweet almond oil to make it vegan)

30 drops lavender essential oil

10 drops eucalyptus essential oil

1 drop geranium essential oil

Combine all ingredients in a foaming pump bottle and shake well.

TO USE Shake well before each use. Lather a small amount onto damp skin with your hands or an exfoliating cloth such as the Hemp exfoliating washcloth (page 151). Rinse well, then pat dry.

MAKES about 12 × 30 ml (1 fl oz) bars

PREP TIME 20 minutes

EQUIPMENT double boiler + 2 silicone cupcake trays

EXFOLIATING COFFEE BODY BARS

These bars are so delicious you will want to eat them! They are basically chocolate and fresh coffee. I love making a batch as a self-care gift for a friend. They are great in the shower to gently exfoliate and moisturise, less wasteful than buying packaged versions, and cleaner and tidier than a jar of body scrub. I like to use these once every month or so to brighten my skin, exfoliate and deeply moisturise. I add lavender essential oil, as it is one of the gentlest and most soothing to the skin, but the oils you add are up to you. I use silicone cupcake trays that have twelve moulds in each, as I think the size is nice and handy, but larger ones work too.

200 g (7 oz) organic cacao butter, grated or finely chopped

90 g (3 oz/¾ cup) coffee grounds, fresh or used and dried

10 drops lavender essential oil

In a double boiler, gently melt the cacao butter over a low heat until melted. Allow it to cool to room temperature. Add the coffee grounds and essential oil and stir well. Pour the mixture into the cupcake trays, then place them in the freezer for a minimum of 1 hour to set. If you live in a warm climate, store any extra bars in an airtight container in the refrigerator to stop them melting.

TO USE Gently massage the bar over damp skin, avoiding your face and neck. Be careful – the residual oil might make your shower a bit slippery. Rinse well and pat dry.

TABLESPOON

MAKES 80 ml (2½ fl oz/⅓ cup)

PREP TIME 2 minutes

EQUIPMENT glass jar or bowl + mixing spoon

FOOT & HAND SCRUB

I don't do this very often, but when I do my hands and feet feel good as new! The light abrasion from the salt and bicarb soda, and the deep moisturisation of the olive oil is a match made in heaven. I like the simple combination of peppermint and lavender to soothe and refresh, but you can play around with your favourite scents. Tea-tree is another great one, as it's both antifungal and antibacterial.

60 ml (2 fl oz/¼ cup) organic cold-pressed olive oil

2 tablespoons salt

1 tablespoon bicarbonate of soda (baking soda)

2 drops peppermint essential oil

2 drops lavender essential oil

Combine all ingredients in your glass jar or bowl and stir well to combine. Store in a cool, dry place.

TO USE Fill a basin with warm water and grab a clean, dry towel. Sit on a chair and put your feet in the basin. Stir the scrub to mix it, then gently scrub 1 tablespoon or more onto your feet and hands, taking your time. Rinse well with warm water and towel dry thoroughly. Be careful about getting up and walking around immediately afterwards; the residual oil might make your feet a bit slippery.

MAKES 500 ml (17 fl oz/2 cups)

PREP TIME 2 minutes

EQUIPMENT funnel + foaming bottle

FOAMING HAND SOAP

This recipe is a good example of how a very small amount of natural ingredients can go a very long way. The foaming attachment on the pump bottle extends this soap even further and helps reduce drips and mess. I enjoy mixing it up and trying different essential oils, but this combination is my favourite so far. Tea-tree is a wonderful natural antiseptic and antibacterial, making it the perfect addition. I am a massive fan of anything citrus and Australian native, but here are some other combinations I have tried and loved: peppermint + lavender, rosemary + eucalyptus, orange + ylang ylang, patchouli + geranium. I keep one of these next to the bathroom sink and one next to the kitchen sink. Sweet almond oil is low scent and very moisturising, but you could use any oil that is liquid at room temperature if you already have it on hand.

85 ml (2¾ fl oz/⅓ cup) pure liquid castile soap

2 tablespoons sweet almond oil (olive and jojoba oil work too)

20 drops lemon essential oil

1 drop tea-tree essential oil

375 ml (12½ fl oz/1½ cups) filtered water

Pour the castile soap and sweet almond oil into your bottle. Add the essential oils, then slowly pour in the filtered water, leaving a couple of centimetres of room at the top.

TO USE Shake well before each use. Pump a couple of times into the palms of your hands and wash with warm water, then rinse clean and dry as normal.

HAND
SOAP

MAKES about 270 ml (9 fl oz)

PREP TIME 10 minutes

EQUIPMENT medium bowl, whisk, immersion blender + glass jar

HAND & BODY CREAM

I really like the natural coconut scent of this rich, creamy, hydrating moisturiser. If you prefer a neutral scent as a base so your essential oils stand out, look for coconut oil that has a low scent or is more refined. I have used sweet almond oil for its low scent and vitamin E content, but if you prefer jojoba oil that works well too. I tend to use this recipe in spring and summer, and the Intense body butter (page 120) in autumn and winter.

125 ml (4 fl oz/½ cup) coconut oil, melted

65 ml (2¼ fl oz/¼ cup) sweet almond or jojoba oil

80 ml (2½ fl oz/⅓ cup) aloe vera gel

1 drop geranium essential oil

Whisk all ingredients in a medium bowl to combine. Place in the freezer for 5–10 minutes, or until the edges start to solidify but the mixture remains soft.

Whip the contents with an immersion blender until white and creamy, pushing down the sides with a spatula to smooth out any clumps. Transfer it to a clean jar with an airtight seal.

TO USE Massage a small amount onto clean skin, then leave it to dry for a minute before dressing.

MAKES about 400 ml (13½ fl oz)

PREP TIME 20 minutes

EQUIPMENT double boiler, whisk, immersion blender + glass jar

INTENSE BODY BUTTER

This super-simple, three-ingredient body butter is highly moisturising, thick and creamy. It melts into your skin – luxurious, nourishing and all natural. The shea butter is rich and deeply moisturising, while the sweet almond oil is high in vitamin E, making it incredibly healing, and has very little scent on its own. When I feel like a change, I swap the sweet almond oil for a cold-pressed olive oil. It is not as low in scent, but it lends this butter a beautiful soft feel. Play around with your favourite essential oils to create your own unique, delicious scent (remembering a little goes a long way). I have kept it simple here with sweet and soothing lavender and just a hint of geranium. Some other favourite additions are a small amount of frankincense or a drop of tea-tree, ylang ylang or wild orange. A jar of this stuff makes a beautiful gift!

180 g (6½ oz/1 cup) shea butter, tightly packed

250 ml (8½ fl oz/1 cup) sweet almond or organic cold-pressed olive oil

20 drops lavender essential oil

4 drops geranium essential oil

Using a double boiler, gently melt the shea butter. Once melted, remove it from the heat and add the sweet almond oil and essential oils. Whisk to combine. Place the mixture in the freezer for 20–30 minutes, or until edges start to harden but it remains soft in the centre.

Whip the mixture with an immersion blender until it turns into a consistent, thick cream. Alternatively, you can transfer the mixture to your blender or small food processor and process on high speed for a few seconds. Transfer to a container or jar and store in a cool, dark place.

TO USE Gently massage onto clean, dry skin as needed.

BODY
BUTTER

Natural Harry
BODY LOVE OIL
DAILY RITUALS
- GROUND AND CONNECT -
ALL NATURAL INGREDIENTS
SHACK

MAKES 100 ml (3½ fl oz)

PREP TIME 2 minutes

EQUIPMENT funnel + amber spray bottle

BODY LOVE OIL

Applying this oil is a beautiful way to spend a moment appreciating the skin you are in. In ancient Ayurvedic tradition, there is a practice called *Abhyanga*, or self-massage, a Sanskrit word that can be translated as both 'oil' and 'love'. It's all about appreciating your body, decreasing stress, increasing circulation and nurturing yourself, among many other things. In traditional Abhyanga you warm the oil gently and apply it to your skin, massaging in circular motions towards the heart. I like using sweet almond oil as it has little scent and is full of vitamin E, which is so fabulous for the skin. I love the simple, grounding combination of lavender and geranium here, but you can experiment with other oils to create a scent of your choice. Oil can be very runny, so storing it in a spray bottle makes for easy application.

100 ml (3½ fl oz) sweet almond or jojoba oil

10 drops lavender essential oil

2 drops geranium essential oil

Combine all ingredients in your spray bottle and shake well to combine. Store in a cool, dark place.

TO USE After showering or bathing, spray a fine layer all over the body, avoiding your face and eyes. Massage into your skin using circular motions. Wait for the oil to soak in before dressing. It doesn't take long and is worth it to ensure you absorb all of that precious, nourishing oil.

MAKES about 190 ml (6½ fl oz)

PREP TIME 10 minutes

EQUIPMENT double boiler, mixing spoon + airtight amber glass jar

VAPOUR RUB

I find this light combination of pure essential oils a welcome aid when I'm feeling poorly. Only very little is needed. I like to rub it on my chest when I have a cold, inhaling the refreshing scent to help clear my head and soothe my senses.

60 ml (2 fl oz/¼ cup) coconut oil

60 g (2 oz) shea butter

40 drops rosemary essential oil

40 drops eucalyptus essential oil

25 drops peppermint essential oil

20 drops lemon essential oil

5 drops lavender essential oil

In a double boiler, melt the coconut oil and shea butter, stirring occasionally, until a liquid forms. Remove it from the heat and allow it to cool for a few minutes. Add the essential oils and mix well. Pour the mixture into an amber glass jar or other clean container and transfer it to the refrigerator to set. Once set, store in a cool, dark place.

TO USE Using the tips of your fingers, gently rub a small amount onto your upper chest. Wash your hands immediately afterwards.

VAPOUR
RUB

FACE
WASH

MAKES about 200 ml (7 fl oz)

PREP TIME 2 minutes

EQUIPMENT funnel + foaming amber pump bottle

FOAMING FACE WASH

Super simple, pure and natural, this face wash is both gentle and moisturising. I love that it cleanses my skin without drying it out. Though you can play around with the essential oils in this recipe, I do recommend sticking to ones that are gentle on the skin. It's not essential that you use a foaming nozzle, but I find that it makes the face wash go much further. On the rare occasion I put makeup on, this face wash works really well to remove any build-up on my skin. For a vegan version, omit the honey or replace with the same amount of sweet almond oil.

3 tablespoons jojoba or sweet almond oil

2 tablespoons filtered water

1 tablespoon pure liquid castile soap

1 tablespoon local honey or sweet almond oil

10 drops lavender essential oil

5 drops tea-tree essential oil

Add all ingredients to your bottle. Shake until they are evenly combined.

TO USE Shake for a few seconds before each use. Pump a small amount into the palm of your hand and massage gently into damp skin, avoiding the eyes. Rinse clean and pat dry with a clean cloth or towel. Follow with a light spray of Natural toner (page 128) and a small amount of Face oil (page 131) or Face moisturiser (page 132).

MAKES 90 ml (3 fl oz)

PREP TIME 2 minutes

EQUIPMENT funnel + spray bottle

NATURAL TONER

Toners tend to be made with dehydrating alcohols and chemicals to help remove oils from the skin. This is not that sort of toner. I was hesitant to include this recipe, as I am a fan of fuss-free self care, but after many a trial recipe I have begun to see the merit in using a quality natural toner. This one is a refreshing, light burst of hydration after cleansing. I wash my face once a day in the shower, give it a little spritz of toner when I hop out, let that dry and then moisturise. It has become a habit I love and, if nothing else, I feel like I am caring for my face a little more and allowing it to age gracefully! This toner makes a lovely gift, as it smells divine and feels like luxury. If you want to get fancy with the essential oils, a drop of geranium, frankincense, rose, Roman chamomile or neroli are all lovely.

2 tablespoons rosewater

2 tablespoons witch hazel

2 teaspoons aloe vera gel

10 drops lavender essential oil

Add all ingredients to your spray bottle and shake well.

TO USE Shake before each use. After cleansing, hold the bottle 20–30 cm (8 in–1 ft) from your face, close your eyes and lightly spray a few times, avoiding your eyes. Allow a few minutes for it to dry before applying Face oil (page 131) or Face moisturiser (page 132).

TONER

MAKES 50 ml (1¾ fl oz)

PREP TIME 2 minutes

EQUIPMENT amber glass bottle with a dropper lid

FACE OIL

I enjoy a minimal skincare routine and wear very little makeup because it keeps my skin happy and saves time. That's why I love this two-ingredient face oil: it doesn't get much simpler! This recipe is all about quality over quantity, and just a tiny drop goes a very long way. With nothing but jojoba oil and a few drops of essential oil, it will keep for longer than the Face moisturiser (page 132) too. I use pure lavender, but if you feel like experimenting with different scents you could also try rose or frankincense, or just one drop of geranium for a delicious floral scent.

50 ml (1¾ fl oz) jojoba or rosehip oil

4 drops lavender essential oil

Combine all ingredients in your bottle, attach the lid and shake well.

TO USE After cleansing your face, put a few drops of oil in the palm of your hand. Spread it lightly over your skin, allowing it a minute to sink in.

MAKES about 65 ml (2 fl oz/¼ cup)

PREP TIME 2 minutes

EQUIPMENT small bowl, spoon, immersion blender + amber glass jar

FACE MOISTURISER

This beautifully light moisturiser doubles as a lovely all-over body moisturiser in the warmer months, allowing your skin to both breathe and be nourished. I find it makes my skin super soft. I make a small amount at a time to ensure freshness and zero waste. Keep in mind that different brands of aloe vera will create varied consistencies in this face cream, so avoid store-bought varieties with lots of additives.

60 ml (2 fl oz/¼ cup) aloe vera gel

2 teaspoons jojoba oil

2 drops lavender essential oil (optional)

In a small bowl, combine all ingredients. Use an immersion blender to whip the mixture until it turns white. Transfer to a clean amber glass jar or bottle. Store in a cool, dark place.

TO USE Apply a small amount to the tips of your fingers and massage onto your face. I like to do this in the warmer months after a light spray of Natural toner (page 128), but I prefer to use the Face oil (page 131) in the cooler months.

MAKES 10 ml (¼ fl oz)

PREP TIME 2 minutes

EQUIPMENT roller or dropper bottle

MAKEUP REMOVER

Possibly the best makeup remover you'll ever find is simply some pure plant oils and a soft cloth. Amazing, huh? No complex concoction of alcohols and astringent agents needed! I have found that storing it in either a roller bottle or a dropper makes this simple recipe even more convenient to use. Washable cotton pads or face cloths/washers work a treat. I simply wash mine with the laundry: once clean, they are ready to use again.

1 teaspoon jojoba oil

1 teaspoon sweet almond oil

Combine the oils in your roller or dropper bottle and shake a little to mix.

TO USE Roll or put a few drops onto a clean, reusable cotton pad and run it across your skin a few times until makeup is removed, making sure to be gentle around the eye area. Follow it up with Foaming face wash (page 127).

MAKES enough for 1 mask

PREP TIME 1 minute

EQUIPMENT ceramic bowl + small spoon

FACE MASK

Cleansing and nourishing, this mask is also super gentle on the skin. Because you make it on the spot, it provides a great opportunity to use some aloe vera fresh from the garden if you happen to have some. The bentonite clay draws out impurities, while the honey and aloe vera moisturise. I only have to do this face mask very occasionally to feel the effects! For a vegan version, replace the honey with jojoba or sweet almond oil.

1½ teaspoons bentonite clay

1 teaspoon local honey or jojoba oil

1 teaspoon aloe vera gel, fresh or store-bought

Mix all ingredients together in a small glass or ceramic bowl with a small wooden or ceramic spoon.

TO USE Using a clean makeup brush, apply the mixture to your face, avoiding the eye area. Leave on for 20–25 minutes, then rinse off with warm water and pat dry using clean face cloth/washer.

CASTILE
SOAP
ALMOND
OIL
SHAMPOO

MAKES about 500 ml (17 fl oz/2 cups)

PREP TIME 10 minutes

EQUIPMENT medium saucepan, mixing spoon, funnel, tea strainer/sieve/paper coffee filter + pump bottle

SHAMPOO

It has taken me years to create an effective natural shampoo. I found that many DIY recipes left something to be desired, and though an apple-cider vinegar rinse after washing does help balance the hair's pH, it couldn't seem to get rid of the residual castile soap left behind. Then I found an amazing ingredient that makes all the difference: shikakai powder. Shikakai derives from the *Acacia concinna*, a climbing shrub, and has been used on the Indian subcontinent since ancient times to clean and strengthen hair, not to mention promote growth and shine. As a natural surfactant, it works to cleanse the hair and remove residue from soap. I love to add rosemary essential oil to this recipe, as it's traditionally used to stimulate hair growth and scalp health. I also like to mix it up sometimes and add a little lavender and/or a drop or two of tea-tree.

315 ml (10½ fl oz/1¼ cups) filtered water

3 teaspoons shikakai powder

125 ml (4 fl oz/½ cup) pure liquid castile soap

3 tablespoons aloe vera gel, or 1 teaspoon powdered

1 tablespoon bicarbonate of soda (baking soda)

2 teaspoons sweet almond oil

20 drops rosemary essential oil

In a medium saucepan, bring the water to boil. Turn off the heat and add the shikakai powder, stirring until completely dissolved. Let it steep until cooled to room temperature. Using a funnel and a tea strainer, sieve or paper coffee filter, strain the shakakai liquid into your pump bottle. Add all other ingredients, seal the lid and shake well. It should keep for up to 2 months, or longer if you use filtered water and powdered aloe vera.

TO USE Shake before each use. Lather a tablespoon or more into wet hair, massaging from the roots down to the ends. Rinse well. Follow with the pH-balancing hair rinse (page 140) and Conditioner & hair mask (page 143) if needed.

MAKES enough for about 20 rinses

PREP TIME none

EQUIPMENT 1 litre (24 fl oz/4 cup) jug (or larger)

PH-BALANCING HAIR RINSE

Apple-cider vinegar is used in natural hair care for many reasons, one of which is the way it helps to balance pH levels. I find that it helps detangle my long hair and remove any shampoo residue. It's also improved the health of my hair and scalp, and my hair's shine to boot. To make the process easy, I keep a one-litre bottle of apple-cider vinegar and a jug in the shower. That way I can easily make up some of this rinse on the spot!

1 litre (34 fl oz/4 cups) apple-cider vinegar

TO USE Keep the container of vinegar near the tub or shower. After shampooing and rinsing your hair, pour roughly 2–3 tablespoons of it into your jug and fill the rest with warm water from the shower or tap. Slowly pour the rinse through wet hair, avoiding the face and eyes. Comb it through before rinsing well. Follow it up with Conditioner & hair mask (page 143) or just dry it as normal.

SHAMPOO
HAIR
RINSE

QUARTER TEASPOON
HALF TEASPOON

MAKES about 160 ml (5½ fl oz)

PREP TIME 5 minutes

EQUIPMENT small saucepan, bowl, whisk, immersion blender + jar

CONDITIONER & HAIR MASK

Surfing, swimming and gardening tends to dry out my hair over time. To counterbalance the damage, I get regular trims and pop this simple hair mask on every month or so. It really moisturises and nourishes the ends of my hair. I also use a small amount as a conditioner every three or so washes for a bit of extra love. Everyone's hair is slightly different, so do a patch test first to make sure it works well for you. I love adding rosemary essential oil to my conditioner to aid hair growth and general health, but you can really play around with your favourite scents or omit essential oils altogether. I also love lavender and tea-tree in this one!

2 tablespoons coconut oil

120 ml (4 fl oz) aloe vera gel

5 drops rosemary essential oil

In a small saucepan, melt the coconut oil, then pour it into a bowl and allow it to cool to room temperature. Add the aloe vera and essential oil and whisk until combined. Using an immersion blender or small food processor, blend until super smooth and creamy. Store in an airtight jar kept in a cool, dry place.

TO USE AS A HAIR MASK Apply it to dry hair in sections, combing it through to the ends. Leave in for 30 minutes–1 hour. Follow with the Shampoo (page 139) and pH-balancing hair rinse (page 140).

TO USE AS A CONDITIONER Apply a small amount to the very ends of wet hair after shampooing or using the pH-balancing hair rinse. Comb through the ends and rinse well under warm water. Dry as normal.

MAKES 30 ml (1 fl oz)

PREP TIME 5 minutes

EQUIPMENT double boiler, fork + small makeup pot

WILD ORANGE & VANILLA LIP BALM

There are so many delicious combinations you can create with this recipe, and this is my favourite. Chocolate and orange are just made to be together. It smells and tastes so yummy you will want to eat it! The cacao and shea butters feel incredibly rich and moisturising, and will leave a little shine on the lips. I love making it in big batches of five or so pots so I have a few on hand to gift friends and family. It is also a wonderful way to repurpose and upcycle small, clean and empty makeup and skincare containers. I love swapping the orange oil for two drops of peppermint oil for a fresh choc-mint version. This recipe also makes a wonderfully rich skin balm: simply double or triple the quantities and swap the essential oils for lavender or geranium.

2 teaspoons shea butter

1 teaspoon cacao butter, finely grated

1 teaspoon coconut oil

10 drops orange essential oil

3 drops vanilla oil

Combine the shea butter, cacao butter and coconut oil in a double boiler and melt gently over a low heat. Remove from the heat and add the orange and vanilla oils. Gently whisk the mixture with a fork to combine evenly. Pour into your small pot and set it on the bench to cool. You may like to stir it a few times as it sets to make sure the ingredients don't separate.

LIPS

MAKES about 210 ml (17½ oz/2 cups)

PREP TIME 5 minutes

EQUIPMENT blender or food processor, medium bowl, wooden spoon + airtight glass jar

OAT & COCONUT BATH SOAK

My skin feels so amazing, moisturised and soft after bathing in this delicious soak. Oats contain compounds called saponins, which are natural cleansers. Their soothing properties, combined with nourishing and moisturising coconut milk, makes a beautiful pampering combination. I have added a touch of bicarb soda for its antibacterial and anti-inflammatory properties, and some relaxing lavender oil to further calm and soothe the skin. The dried flowers aren't critical, but do add a nice touch, especially when making this soak as a gift. I have used dried cornflower in this batch, but I also love rose petals and lavender.

100 g (3½ oz/1 cup) organic rolled oats

55 g (2 oz/½ cup) coconut milk powder

50 g (1¾ oz/¼ cup) bicarbonate of soda (baking soda)

20 drops lavender essential oil

2 tablespoons dried flowers (optional)

Using your food processor or blender, grind the oats into a fine powder. Transfer them to a bowl and add the coconut milk powder, bicarb soda, essential oil and dried flowers. Stir well and store in an airtight glass jar.

TO USE Add ¼–½ cup to a warm running bath and stir well. Soak for 20 minutes or more. Rinse off and pat the skin dry.

MAKES 300 g (10½ oz/2 cups)

PREP TIME 2 minutes

EQUIPMENT large bowl, wooden spoon + airtight glass jar

MAGNESIUM BATH SOAK

Any soak in the bath is relaxing, grounding and peaceful. To really take it to the next level, add some magnesium flakes and a few drops of your favourite essential oils. These beautiful, natural ingredients can help relieve muscle soreness and tension. Yes, please! You can find dried flowers at many health food and wholefoods stores, and they make a very pretty addition. If you don't have magnesium flakes on hand, Epsom salts work well too.

300 g (10½ oz/2 cups) magnesium flakes or Epsom salts

30 drops essential oils of choice

2 tablespoons dried flowers (optional)

In a large bowl, combine all ingredients and stir well. Transfer them to a large jar or container for storage.

TO USE Dissolve ½ cup in warm water as you run your bath. Swish it around before soaking for 20 minutes or more. Enjoy!

45
33
0
THE
MOONFLOWE
MONOLOGUES

MAKES one 15 × 15 cm (6 × 6 in) washcloth

EQUIPMENT about 25 metres (82 feet) of 1 mm (<⅛ in) thick hemp twine + 6 mm (¼ in) knitting needles

HEMP EXFOLIATING WASHCLOTH

If you have some knitting needles and a ball of hemp twine handy, this is a wonderful way to make yourself a natural exfoliating washcloth for the shower or bath. It is natural and durable, and it lathers up really nicely with soap or body wash. Making one or two to go with a gift of body wash really completes an already thoughtful present. If you are feeling really fancy, you can make a couple of these and stitch them together on three sides to create a soap saver. This isn't a knitting book, but you'll find plenty of how-to videos online to help, and this project is a great one for beginners to try. Choose your knitting needles according to the thickness of your hemp. The thicker the needles, the more open the weave and the more movement you will get in the cloth.

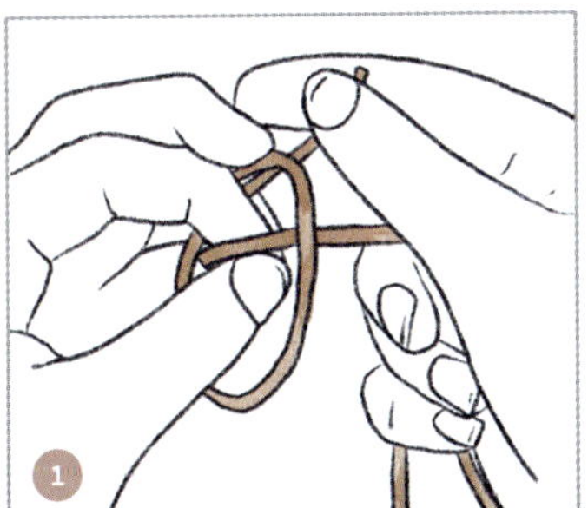

Casting on: Create a slip knot: loop the end of the hemp around your fingers and pull another loop through the first loop.

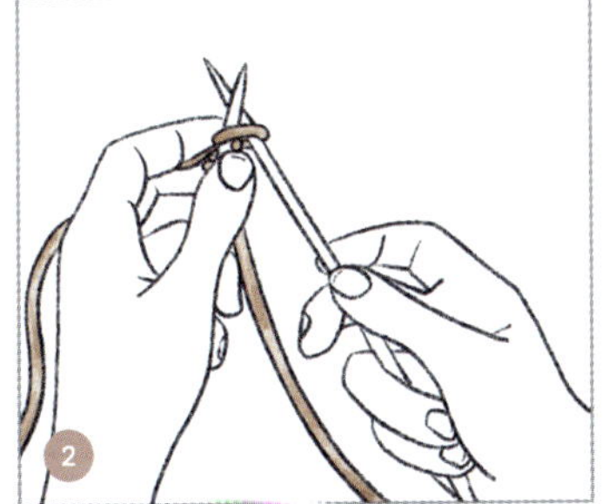

Casting on: Slip your slip-knot loop loosely around one needle. Hold the short tail of the hemp along the left-hand needle, out of the way. Thread the right-hand needle upwards through the slip knot behind the left-hand needle, creating an X with the two needles.

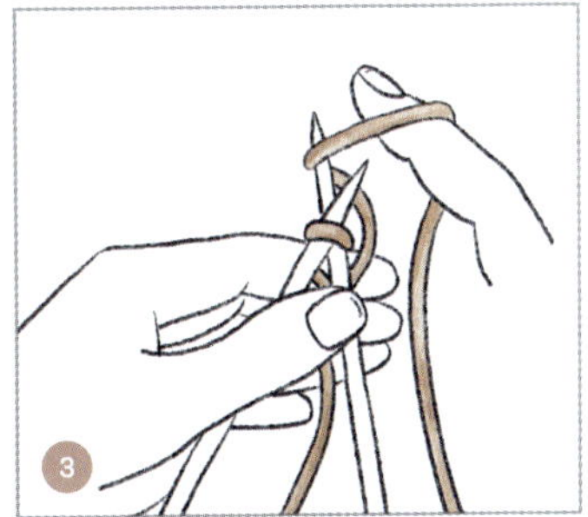

Casting on: Take the working hemp (the one attached to your ball of hemp) in your right hand and loop it around the right-hand needle from back to front and then down between the two needles. Be careful not to collect the left-hand needle in the process.

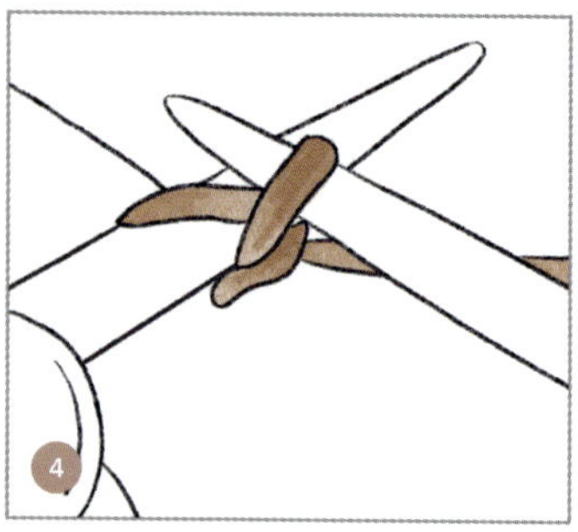

Casting on: Holding the hemp down on the right-hand needle, pull the right-hand needle down and through the hemp, hooking the middle thread onto the right-hand needle (this thread will become the loop). Push the right-hand needle up until your loop is long enough for the tip of the left-hand needle to reach it.

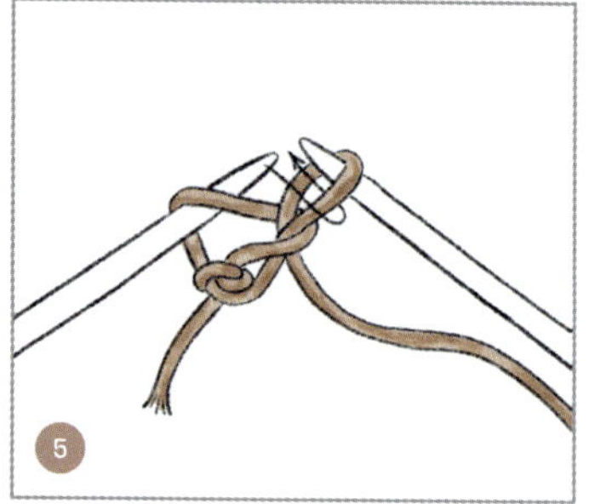

Casting on: Poke the left-hand needle through the back of the new loop on the right-hand needle. Slide the right-hand needle out and gently pull on the hemp. The loop (your first stitch!) is now on your left-hand needle. Using your newly formed stitch as the starting point each time, repeat steps 2–5 until you have cast twenty stitches.

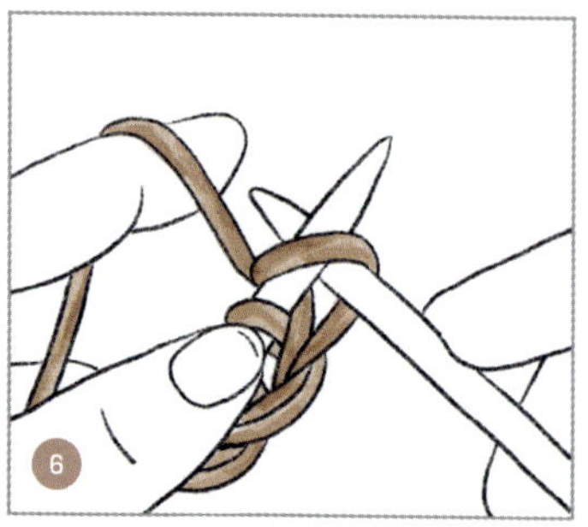

Knitting: Hold the working hemp and the needle with the cast-on stitches in your left hand. Thread the right-hand needle through the top loop on the left-hand needle from underneath, resting it behind the left needle to form an X.

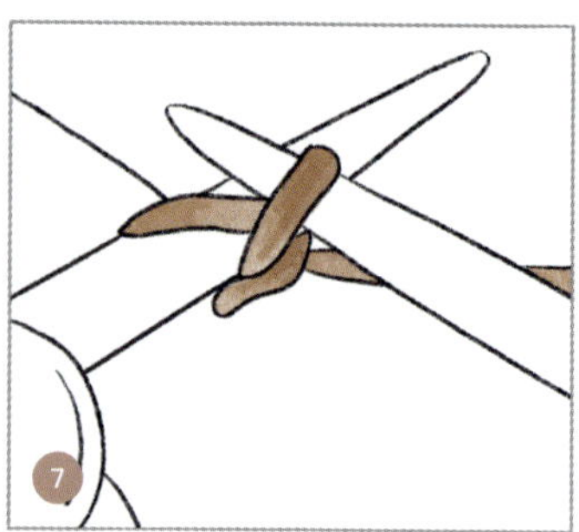

Knitting: Take the working hemp in your right hand and loop it around the right-hand needle from back to front and then down between the two needles.

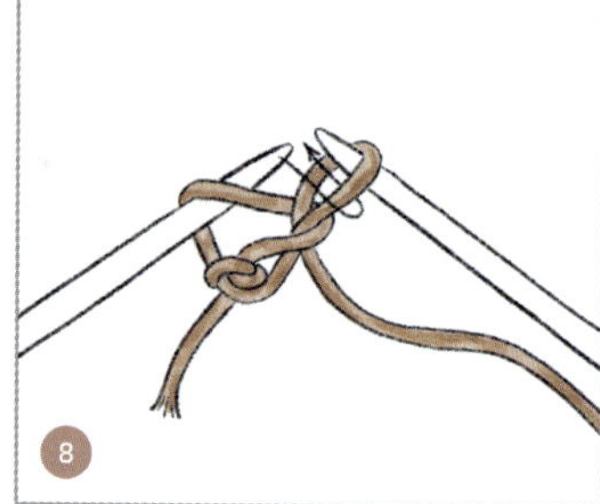

Knitting: Keeping the working hemp pulled tight, pull the right-hand needle towards you, collecting the stitch through the loop.

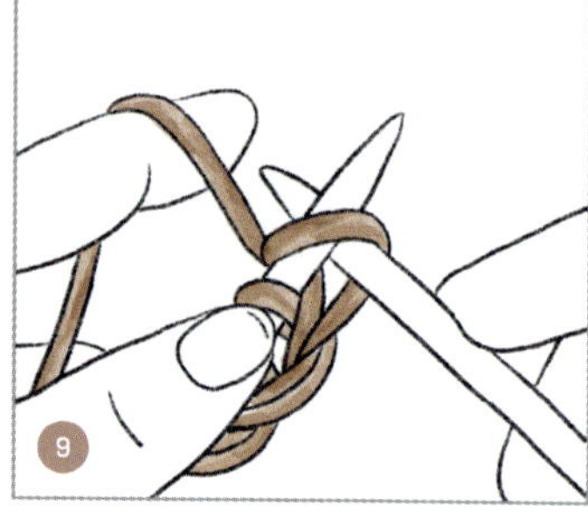

Knitting: You now have a new stitch on the right-hand needle. Pull the right-hand needle up and away from you until the old cast-on stitch at the top of the left-hand needle has slid off. You have now knitted your first stitch. Repeat steps 6–9 until there are no stitches left on the left-hand needle.

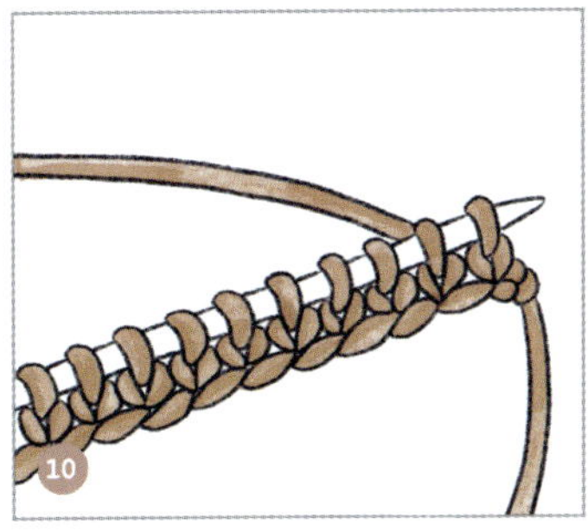

Knitting: Swap the needles between your hands so the needle with your stitches is in your left hand, and the free needle is in your right hand. Repeat steps 6–9 until you have completed forty rows, swapping the needles between your hands once you've completed each row.

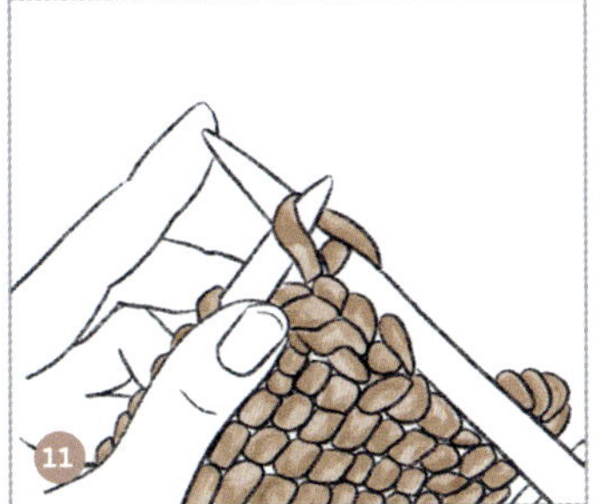

Casting off: Start by knitting two stitches onto the right-hand needle. Using the left-hand needle, pick up the lower stitch and pull it over the higher stitch. Drop it so there is only one stitch remaining on the right-hand needle.

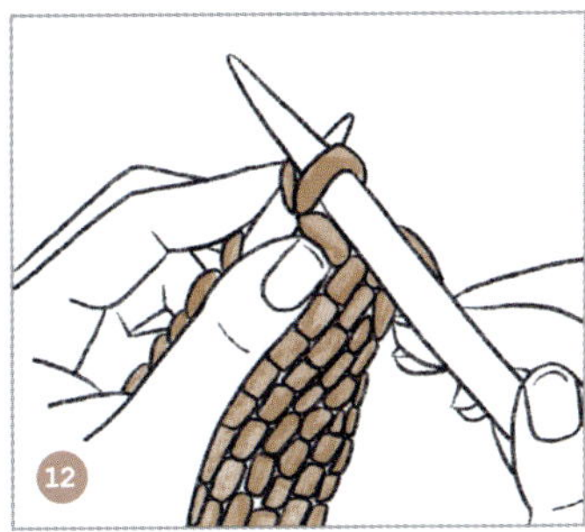

Casting off: Knit another stitch and repeat step 11 as you work your way down the row. When there is only one stitch left on the right-hand needle, cut off the working hemp about 10 cm (4 in) from the knitted section.

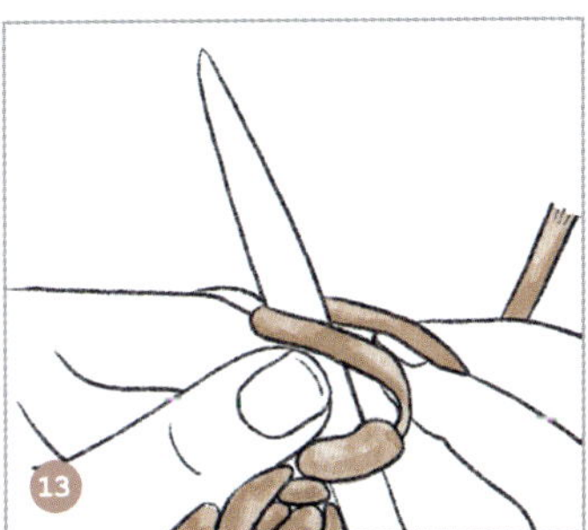

Casting off: Loop the hemp tail around your needle, then pull the stitch over the hemp tail.

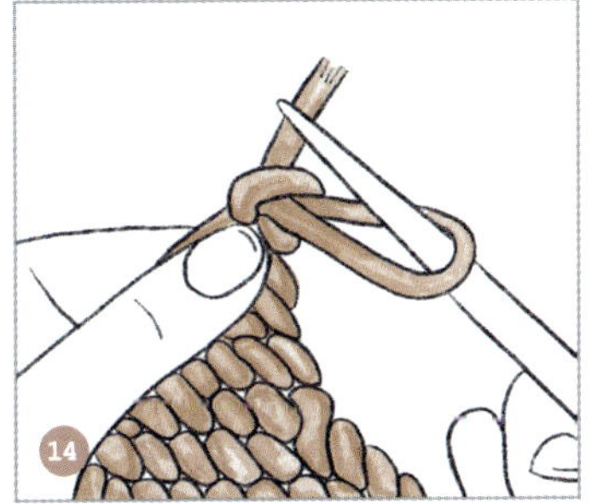

Casting off: Pull the hemp tail through the needle.

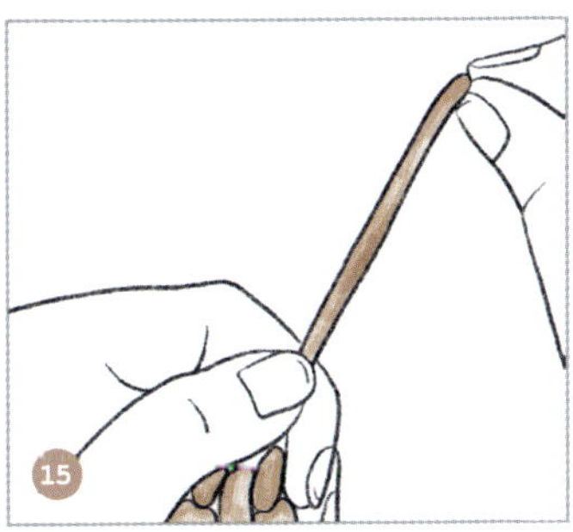

Casting off: Pull to tighten, then weave in the loose ends (use a darning needle to sew the loose end down the side of the washcloth). You are done!

PERFUME, THREE WAYS

Nothing beats natural when it comes to scents. Beautiful, clean scents from a fragrance made with pure plant extracts and no chemical nasties certainly stands out from the rest! And they need not smell like a hippie shop of yesteryear. You can create the most clean and gorgeous fragrances with just a few simple ingredients. The following are my easy DIY tips and suggestions for creating your own perfect blend. I have also shared my personal perfume blends, both a simple version and a more complex one. Take it as an invitation to play around and make a unique scent you love; keep it nice and simple with just one to three essential oils or try a more complex blend. I suggest testing the oils together by holding a couple at a time under your nose to see if you like the combination. Or better yet, add a drop of each into a bowl or the bottom of your roller bottle, spray bottle or pot and adjust until you are happy with the combination. I love giving these sprays, rollers and balms as gifts.

SCENT SUGGESTIONS

TOP NOTES (FRESH):

This scent will reach your senses first.

bergamot, grapefruit, lavender, lemon, lime, neroli, rosemary, sweet orange

MIDDLE NOTES (SWEET):

The warmth and heart of your perfume. These linger most.

chamomile, cinnamon, geranium, honeysuckle, jasmine, juniper, melissa, rose, rosemary, ylang ylang

BASE NOTES (EARTHY):

You may not smell these first off, but they will evolve over time.

cedarwood, frankincense, patchouli, vanilla, vetiver

To make your unique blend, start by selecting your base note(s), then move on to your middle note(s) and finally your top note(s). I like to start with one drop of each to test whether I like the combination and build the scent from there. As you build, follow this ratio.

TOP: 30% MIDDLE: 50% BASE: 20%

MY FAVOURITES

SIMPLE BLEND

20 drops ylang ylang

12 drops orange

4 drops patchouli

4 drops vanilla oil

MORE COMPLEX BLEND

15 drops ylang ylang

8 drops orange

5 drops vanilla

4 drops lavender

2 drops cinnamon

2 drops rosemary

1 drop patchouli

1 drop rose geranium

MAKES 2 × 20 ml (¾ fl oz) balms

PREP TIME 15 minutes

EQUIPMENT 2 bowls, double boiler, spoon + 2 perfume pots with airtight lids

PERFUME BALM

This is a very compact, convenient way to take your natural perfume with you wherever you go. I find it perfect for travel. I like to apply it to my pulse points and the back of my neck for a subtle, yummy scent. It is also a great way to repurpose finished lip balm and eye cream pots – just make sure to clean everything well first. For a vegan version, replace the beeswax with half the amount of candelilla wax.

2 teaspoons beeswax, pastilles or grated, or 1 teaspoon candelilla wax

1 tablespoon sweet almond oil

30–40 drops essential oils of choice

Gently heat the beeswax in a double boiler until it turns liquid. Add the sweet almond oil and stir to combine. Remove the beeswax from the heat and add your essential oils. Stir to combine, then pour the mixture into the pots. Set them on the bench to cool completely before screwing the lids on.

TO USE Gently melt a small amount between your fingers and apply a little to your pulse points.

MAKES 10 ml (¼ fl oz)

PREP TIME 2 minutes

EQUIPMENT roller bottle

PERFUME ROLLER

Roller bottles are another great, compact way to take your perfume with you anywhere. I love how convenient the roller bottle makes it to apply! To ensure that the beautiful scent of the essential oils shines through, use a carrier oil with a low scent such as jojoba, sweet almond or fractionated coconut (the kind that stays liquid at room temperature). I like sweet almond oil, as it is very low in its own natural scent and comes from minimal processing. It's important to try to find roller bottles with metal (stainless steel) balls, as the oil in the perfume can cause plastic to leach chemicals. Always apply your roller to clean skin and do a patch test first.

30–40 essential oils of choice

2 teaspoons sweet almond or jojoba oil

⅛ teaspoon dried rose petals, lavender or cornflower (optional)

Add your chosen blend of essential oils to your roller bottle. Carefully fill the remaining space with your chosen carrier oil, and dried flowers if using, before attaching the roller ball and lid and shaking well.

TO USE Roll onto clean skin on any pulse points.

CLEAN &
SMOOTH
VODKA

MAKES 100 ml (3½ fl oz)

PREP TIME 2 minutes

DEVELOPMENT TIME 48 hours (and up to 6 weeks)

EQUIPMENT jar with lid, funnel, paper coffee filter + amber spray bottle

PERFUME SPRAY

Here's a simple way to make a very potent, yet natural perfume in its most traditional form: a spray. If you are sensitive to alcohol on the skin, you can omit it, but it's there to help disperse the oil's scent, increase its strength and preserve the perfume. Its strength will increase and develop over time, so I like to leave the finished product in a cool, dark place for a couple of weeks before using it. However, you can also spray it on straightaway. I like to lightly mist it over my lower neck and the insides of my wrists. It smells amazing, and I always receive lovely comments.

30–40 drops essential oils of choice

3 tablespoons organic vodka

1 tablespoon sweet almond oil

1 tablespoon filtered water

In a small jar, blend the essential oils, then add the vodka and sweet almond oil. Seal the lid and set the bottle aside in a cool, dark place for a minimum of 48 hours. The scent will strengthen with age, and you can leave to it to develop for up to 6 weeks.

Once developed, shake the mixture and pour it through a paper coffee filter into the spray bottle. Add the filtered water, attach the lid, and shake vigorously for a few minutes.

TO USE Shake well before each use. Spray your perfume about 20 cm (8 in) from your body onto pulse points, avoiding your face.

BUG REPEL

MAKES 200 ml (7 fl oz)

PREP TIME 2 minutes

EQUIPMENT amber spray bottle + funnel

There are many pure essential oils that naturally deter mosquitoes and other small bugs. Why not use them instead of harsh, foul-smelling chemicals? The beauty of this recipe is that the scent develops and becomes stronger over time. I keep mine at the front door for easy access and take it when we go on camping adventures. I also love making these as gifts. They smell amazing, are super useful and look lovely. You can add a couple of drops of clove and cinnamon for a festive, warm scent if you have some on hand.

100 ml (3½ fl oz) witch hazel

80 ml (2½ fl oz/⅓ cup) filtered water

1 tablespoon organic vodka

20 drops lemon essential oil

20 drops lavender essential oil

10 drops rosemary essential oil

7 drops lemongrass essential oil

5 drops eucalyptus essential oil

3 drops vanilla oil

Combine all ingredients in the spray bottle. Attach the lid and shake well.

TO USE Shake well before each use, as the mixture will separate over time. Hold the bottle 20 cm (8 in) or more away from your body and spray a light mist over exposed areas, avoiding the face and eyes.

BUG
REPEL

ZINC
BARS

MAKES 180 g (6½ oz) or 12 small bars

PREP TIME 10 minutes

EQUIPMENT double boiler, mixing spoon + silicone cupcake trays

ZINC SUN BARS

Sun safety is paramount, especially where I live in the southern hemisphere. I like to stay covered and in the shade whenever possible, but when I know I'll be in the sun I regularly apply these zinc bars to any exposed skin. Zinc oxide is a naturally occurring mineral that provides more than twenty-five times the skin's natural protection against harmful UVA & UVB rays. Mixed with a simple combination of natural butters, it helps smooth the zinc over the skin and moisturise at the same time. I have found that it leaves very little white residue, unlike many natural zinc sunscreen products. When I am surfing or swimming for a longer period, I make sure to put it on thick for better protection. It helps that these bars make for convenient, easy application, but they will melt in high heat. I like to store mine in a small tin in case I am caught out on a particularly warm day!

85 g (3 oz/1 cup) cacao butter, finely chopped

60 g (2 oz/½ cup) shea butter

1 tablespoon coconut oil

2 teaspoons cacao powder (optional, adjust for tint)

2 tablespoons zinc oxide (non-nano)

10 drops lavender essential oil (optional for scent)

In a double boiler, combine the cacao and shea butters, coconut oil and cacao powder and melt over a low heat. Remove from the heat and add the zinc and essential oil, stirring every so often as it cools. Take care not to inhale the zinc oxide!

Pour the mixture into the trays and freeze for about 20 minutes.

Store any excess bars in the refrigerator. This cream is not waterproof and will need to be reapplied after swimming and/or sweating.

MAKES 100 ml (3½ fl oz)

PREP TIME 2 minutes

EQUIPMENT funnel + amber spray bottle

SUMMER SUN SOOTHING MIST

I believe the best sun protection is being sensible about your exposure. Covering up and keeping in the shade is ideal, but I love activities like surfing and swimming that keep me out in the sun. I first made this little concoction one evening after a tad too much time in the surf! The cooling, soothing blend of peppermint, aloe and lavender helped calm and moisturise my skin. Aloe vera has been used for centuries to accelerate the healing of burns, so this combo is an absolute dream. I've added some rose water too, as it is just so gentle and beautiful on the skin, plus it smells divine.

50 ml (1¾ fl oz) aloe vera gel

50 ml (1¾ fl oz) pure rose water

20 drops lavender essential oil

4 drops peppermint essential oil

Add all ingredients to your spray bottle and shake well to combine.

TO USE Shake well before each use. Simply spray a light layer over sun-kissed areas, always avoiding your eyes. Allow it to air dry and repeat every so often to prolong that soothing, cooling feeling.

ALOE
SUMMER

FOOD

This chapter includes some of my favourite pantry staples to make at home. Making things like milk, crackers and bread from scratch means they'll contain the best quality ingredients: no preservatives and additives you can't even pronounce. Plus, they are way more economical and help you avoid needless packaging. That's a satisfying thing in an age when it's nearly impossible to buy these things in stores without finding them wrapped in plastic. Take it to the next level by growing your own herbs and vegetables, composting your food scraps or making them into vegetable stock. You'll be amazed by how such small steps reduce the rubbish your household creates.

TOOLS

- Pyrex containers, or any glass food storage containers you like
- Airtight glass jars of varying sizes, with lids
- High-speed blender or food processor
- Immersion blender
- Whisk
- Wooden spoons
- Compostable baking paper
- Beeswax wraps

SHOPPING LIST

- Apple-cider vinegar
- Baking powder
- Coconut milk, cream and desiccated coconut
- Dried herbs and spices
- Dried legumes, such as lentils and chickpeas
- Garlic powder
- Oats
- Brown rice
- Quinoa
- Buckwheat
- Pure maple syrup
- Medjool dates
- Nutritional yeast
- Nuts, such as almonds and cashews
- Quality salt (I use pink sea salt)
- Seeds such as chia, flax and sunflower
- Tahini, hulled
- Tamari and/or coconut aminos

SAUERKRAUT

MAKES about 1 litre (34 fl oz/4 cups)

PREP TIME 20 minutes

FERMENTATION TIME 5 days

EQUIPMENT chopping board, sharp knife, large mixing bowl, mixing spoon + large sterilised glass jar with lid

To put it simply, sauerkraut (or sour cabbage) is fermented cabbage. The health benefits of this traditional German side dish are amazing, from improving digestion to boosting immunity. It stores incredibly well in an airtight container when kept in the refrigerator and is a healthy addition to any savoury dish. These two are my favourite flavours. I rarely eat a salad, nourish bowl or avocado on toast without a spoonful of either.

APPLE & DILL

1 large green cabbage, finely shredded, saving 2 large leaves

4 large green apples, peeled and grated

40 g (1½ oz/¼ cup) fresh dill, finely chopped

3 tablespoons caraway seeds

80 g (2¾ oz/¼ cup) good-quality salt

BEETROOT & GINGER

1 large green cabbage, finely shredded, saving 2 large leaves

3 large beetroot, peeled and grated

1 tablespoon peeled grated ginger

80 g (2¾ oz/¼ cup) good-quality salt

Sterilise a chopping board, sharp knife, large mixing bowl, wooden spoon and large glass jars with hot, soapy water and rinse clean before drying.

Choose which version you'd like to make. Remove the outer leaves of the cabbage before shredding it, remembering to set aside two leaves. Combine all ingredients of whichever version you're making in a large mixing bowl and massage them with your hands for about 10 minutes. Really squeeze the mixture as you go. A liquid will begin to form at the bottom of the bowl, and this brine should be almost level with the veggies when you are finished.

Cover and leave to rest for 1½ hours before scooping it into your sterilised jar, leaving at least 3 cm (1¼ in) of room at the top. Top with the reserved cabbage leaves. Using a clean shot glass or something like it, gently push the cabbage leaves down until the brine rises over the solids. Secure the lid and leave it to ferment in a dry place at room temperature for approximately 5 days before storing in the refrigerator, where it will keep for several months.

MAKES 3 × 500 ml (17 fl oz/2 cups) jars

PREP TIME 25 minutes

FERMENTATION TIME at least 24 hours

EQUIPMENT chopping board, sharp knife, saucepan + 3 airtight glass jars

QUICK PICKLED VEGGIES

This is such a delicious way to use up those last few veggies from the bottom of the fridge! Waste not, want not. Add them to a burger, a nourish bowl or on top of some avocado on Oaty seed loaf (page 186). The beauty of this recipe is that you can customise it to suit what you have on hand. My favourite veggies to pickle are cucumber, zucchini, cauliflower, carrot, radish, onion, garlic, peppers, asparagus, green beans and eggplant. My favourite herbs and spices to add in are dill, thyme, mustard seeds, chilli flakes, coriander and fennel seeds.

about 600 g (1 lb 5 oz/6 cups) raw vegetables, washed and peeled (if necessary)

½ brown or red onion, peeled and sliced

2 tablespoons spices and dried or fresh herbs

750 ml (25½ fl oz/3 cups) apple-cider vinegar

500 ml (17 fl oz/2 cups) filtered water

2 tablespoons good-quality salt

3 tablespoons coconut sugar

Sterilise your jars with hot, soapy water and rinse clean before drying.

Cut your vegetables into pieces as desired.

Add the vegetables, onion and herbs and spices to your jars and pack them down tightly, leaving 2.5 cm (1 in) of room at the top.

In a medium saucepan, bring the apple-cider vinegar, water, salt and coconut sugar to the boil. Turn off the heat and carefully pour the hot mixture into the jars, making sure to fully submerge the vegetables while leaving 2–3 cm (¾–1¼ in) of room at the top. Lightly tap the bottom of the jars on the bench a few times to release any trapped air.

Place the lids on the jars and transfer them to the refrigerator. Leave them there for a minimum of 24 hours, allowing the flavour to develop. They will keep in the refrigerator for up to 3 weeks.

PLANT-BASED MILK, THREE WAYS

Making plant-based milks at home is very satisfying. Whipping them up yourself comes with many perks: you can use the leftover nutmeal in other recipes, cut out added sugars and preservatives AND avoid buying single-use plastics. You can make them from many different ingredients: rice, coconut, hemp, oat, quinoa, macadamia nuts, cashews, almonds and hazelnuts. My favourites are almond, oat and coconut. Oat milk is so versatile. It froths really well in coffee and it is very cost effective. Nut milks have a wonderful flavour and creamy consistency. Coconut milk, with its distinct flavour, makes a delicious addition to smoothies, curries and soups. Making your own plant-based milk is simple – all you need is the raw ingredients and some water!

MAKES 1 litre (34 fl oz/4 cups)

PREP TIME 5 minutes

SOAKING TIME 8 hours

EQUIPMENT large bowl, sieve, high-speed blender, nut-milk bag + sterilised airtight glass bottle with lid

NUT MILK

You can make milk from almost any kind of nut and some seeds. My favourites are the nuts with the mildest flavour, such as almonds and cashews (though hazelnuts and macadamia nuts are also lovely). Their mild, nutty flavour makes them very versatile, as the subtle flavour doesn't compete for attention. Soaking nuts overnight not only softens them, making them easy to blend, but also removes phytic acid and enzyme inhibitors, making for smoother digestion. When I make almond milk, I often save the pulp and use it straightaway to make energy bars and bliss bites. I also turn it into almond flour for later use; just spread it on a tray lined with baking paper and bake at 100°C (200°F) for two hours, stirring every thirty minutes until it is completely dried out. Let it cool completely before blending on high speed until a powdery flour forms. Voila!

around 150 g (5½ oz/1 cup) raw nuts (I use almonds)

1 litre (34 fl oz/4 cups) filtered water

1 tablespoon pure maple syrup or 2 Medjool dates, pitted

1 pinch good-quality salt

OPTIONAL EXTRAS FOR FLAVOUR

½ cup fresh strawberries or raspberries

1 tablespoon cacao powder

1 teaspoon vanilla powder

Soak the nuts in water overnight or for a minimum of 8 hours. Once soaked, drain them and rinse well. Transfer them to your blender or food processor and add all the other ingredients, including any optional extras. Blend for 30 seconds on high speed. Pour the blended mixture into your nut-milk bag and squeeze the liquid out into a bowl. Don't throw out your leftover meal (see my suggestion above)! Store the fresh milk in a clean, airtight glass bottle in the refrigerator for up to 1 week.

Shake well before each use. This milk has no preservatives, so it will separate over time.

MAKES 1 litre (34 fl oz/4 cups)

PREP TIME 5 minutes

EQUIPMENT high-speed blender, thin clean cloth or nut-milk bag, large bowl + sterilised airtight glass bottle with lid

OAT MILK

There is no soaking required to make oat milk. Just pop the ingredients into your blender and away you go! I love adding it to smoothies and porridge, and it froths really well in coffee. The neutral flavour lends itself to many recipes and it is extremely cost effective: just one cup of oats makes a litre of milk with all-compostable waste. You can use a nut-milk bag to strain this milk, but I do find that a close-woven cloth like cotton jersey works best to achieve a really smooth, creamy milk.

1 litre (34 fl oz/4 cups) filtered water

100 g (3½ oz/1 cup) organic rolled oats

1 tablespoon pure maple syrup or 1 Medjool date, pitted

1 pinch good-quality salt

OPTIONAL EXTRAS FOR FLAVOUR

½ cup fresh strawberries or raspberries

1 tablespoon cacao powder

1 teaspoon vanilla powder

Add all ingredients to your food processor or blender and blend at high speed for about 30 seconds. Using a clean cloth, strain the liquid into a large bowl. Pour the milk into the glass bottle and store in the refrigerator, where it will keep for 5–7 days.

Shake well before each use. This milk has no preservatives, so it will separate over time.

MAKES 750 ml (25½ fl oz/3 cups)

PREP TIME 5 minutes

EQUIPMENT high-speed blender, nut-milk bag, large bowl + sterilised airtight glass bottle with lid

COCONUT MILK

You can make this milk using a fresh coconut, but most of us aren't lucky enough to have them growing nearby. That is why I love making coconut milk from shredded or desiccated coconut, which is such an easy staple to keep on hand. In a perfect world we would use only ingredients that grow in our backyard, but I think this version of packaging-free coconut milk is a big step in the right direction. Give it a go and see what you think! It's delicious in smoothies, curries and soups.

750 ml (25½ fl oz/3 cups) filtered water

100 g (3½ oz/2 cups) shredded coconut or coconut chips

1 Medjool date, pitted, or 1 tablespoon pure maple syrup

1 pinch good-quality salt

OPTIONAL EXTRAS FOR FLAVOUR

½ cup fresh strawberries or raspberries

1 tablespoon cacao powder

1 teaspoon vanilla powder

Combine all ingredients in a high-speed blender and blend on high speed for about 2 minutes. Using a nut-milk bag, strain the liquid into a large bowl. Use the pulp to make bliss bites and slices, add to cookies, or put it in the compost. Pour your coconut milk into an airtight bottle or other container and store in the refrigerator, where it will keep for up to 5 days.

Shake well before each use. This milk has no preservatives, so it will separate over time.

COCONUT YOGHURT

MAKES 750 ml (25½ fl oz/3 cups)

PREP TIME 5 minutes

FERMENTATION TIME 24 hours

EQUIPMENT high-speed blender + sterilised glass jar with lid

Coconut yoghurt is a fabulous plant-based alternative to dairy yoghurt. It is widely available at supermarkets and stores, but more often than not it comes in a single-use plastic container. Luckily, it's super easy to make yourself! I love to make a batch in summer when there is more fruit in season to enjoy with this rich, creamy yoghurt. My favourite dish to serve it with is the Buckwheat granola (page 190), paired with fresh fruit and a drizzle of maple syrup.

750 ml (25½ fl oz/3 cups) full-fat canned coconut milk, or freshly made

2 dairy-free probiotic capsules or coconut yoghurt starter

1 tablespoon pure maple syrup (optional)

Put all ingredients in your blender. Blend for a few seconds until well combined.

Pour the mixture into your jar, leaving at least 4–5 cm (1½–2 in) of room at the top: I find the yoghurt expands a little as it ferments. Rest the lid on top rather than securing it to allow air to circulate.

Leave the jar in a warm place (20–25°C/70–77°F) for 24 hours. After about 12 hours, give the yoghurt a stir.

Once the yoghurt has become thick and creamy (if you taste it, it should have a slight tang), seal and refrigerate. It will thicken a bit more once it's chilled. If you would like a thicker, Greek-style yoghurt, substitute half the coconut milk for coconut cream.

MAKES 175 g (6 oz/1 cup)

PREP TIME 2 minutes

EQUIPMENT food processor or high-speed blender + airtight container

PLANT-BASED PARMESAN

This recipe is one of my most-used staples. It adds a delicious flavour to almost any meal, especially pizza, pasta and any Mexican-inspired dish. It is easy to whip up with dry ingredients from your local bulk wholefoods store and it keeps for a long time. I love taking it on camping trips too, as it travels well. You can make it with a number of different nuts and seeds, such as sunflower seeds, Brazil nuts, cashews, almonds and macadamia nuts. Go nuts!

155 g (5½ oz/1 cup) raw nuts (I use cashews)

20 g (¾ oz/⅓ cup) nutritional yeast

1 teaspoon garlic powder

1 teaspoon good-quality salt

Add all ingredients to a food processor and pulse on high speed until you achieve a grainy, even texture. Transfer to an airtight container and store in the refrigerator. Eat within 3 weeks, or you can freeze it for up to 3 months.

MAKES 1 large loaf

PREP TIME 5 minutes

COOK TIME 1 hour

EQUIPMENT 2 bowls, mixing spoon, standard loaf tin, baking paper, spatula, knife + cooling rack

OATY SEED LOAF

No 'airy fairy' bread here. This loaf of hearty, tasty, seeded goodness is yummy and so easy to make. No waiting for the dough to rise, no yeast, refined flours or oil. You can also make it into rolls and bake individual buns. I like to slice mine and store it in the freezer so I always have some on hand. This hearty bread is super satisfying toasted and served with soup, used as a roll for a veggie burger or topped with jam. For a nourishing fruit loaf, add dried fruit and spices. For banana bread, add a couple of ripe mashed bananas. For a savoury bread, add some fresh rosemary, sliced olives and garlic. So versatile!

300 g (10½ oz/3 cups) organic rolled oats

80 g (2¾ oz/½ cup) chia seeds

80 g (2¾ oz/½ cup) pumpkin seeds (pepitas)

70 g (2½ oz/½ cup) sunflower seeds

70 g (2½ oz/½ cup) sesame seeds

40 g (1½ oz/½ cup) psyllium husk

2 tablespoons flaxseeds (linseeds)

1 teaspoon high-quality salt

1 teaspoon baking powder

1 tablespoon pure maple syrup

500 ml (17 fl oz/2 cups) warm filtered water

Preheat your oven to 180°C (350°F).

In a large bowl, combine the dry ingredients and mix well.

In a small bowl, stir the maple syrup and warm water together, then add to the dry ingredients and mix well. Let stand for a few minutes.

Line a loaf tin with baking paper. Pour in the batter, spreading it evenly with a spatula. Bake for 30 minutes. Remove it from the tin, flip it upside down and bake for another 30–40 minutes until it forms a hard crust and a knife inserted comes out clean. Leave it to cool on a cooling rack for 1 hour before slicing. Store in the refrigerator, where it will keep for up to 1 week.

MAKES about 350 g (12½ oz) crackers

PREP TIME 10 minutes

COOK TIME 30–35 minutes

EQUIPMENT large pot, food processor, baking paper, rolling pin, 3 baking trays, cooling racks + airtight container or large glass jar

CRACKERS

Crackers are one of the few things you can't buy without packaging, and they often contain excessive vegetable oils and salt. This wholefood alternative is the perfect homemade cracker, and can be easily adapted to suit your taste. Store in an airtight container and they will keep for up to a month.

110 g (4 oz/½ cup) brown rice

100 g (3½ oz/½ cup) quinoa

750 ml (25½ fl oz/3 cups) + 1 tablespoon filtered water

50 g (1¾ oz/⅓ cup) sesame seeds

60 g (2 oz/⅓ cup) flaxseeds (linseeds)

40 g (1½ oz/¼ cup) chia seeds

1 teaspoon good-quality salt

1 tablespoon dried herbs of choice (I like parsley, basil, cracked pepper, rosemary, thyme and oregano)

½ teaspoon garlic powder (optional)

Preheat your oven to 180°C (350°F).

Rinse the rice and quinoa thoroughly, then add them to a large pot with the 3 cups of water. Bring it to the boil, then reduce to a simmer and cook until the water is absorbed and the grains are sticking together. Turn the heat off and cover, allowing them to cool a little. Transfer to your food processor, add the remaining ingredients and the extra tablespoon of water and pulse until a rough dough forms.

Divide the mixture into thirds and place each third onto a piece of baking paper. Place another piece of baking paper over each and, using a rolling pin, roll out as thinly as possible (aim for 1–2 mm/<⅛ in).

Remove the top sheet of baking paper and transfer the rolled-out dough to three baking trays. Bake for 20 minutes. Remove the trays from the oven and use the spare sheet of baking paper to flip each cracker sheet. Return to the oven for a further 10–15 minutes, until they crisp up and curl at the edges.

Remove the cracker sheets from the oven and transfer to cooling racks. Once they have cooled completely, break into chunks and store in an airtight container.

MAKES 650 g (1 lb 7 oz/5 cups)

PREP TIME 10 minutes

COOK TIME 20 minutes

EQUIPMENT large mixing bowl, wooden spoon, 2 large baking trays, baking paper, cooling racks + airtight jar

BUCKWHEAT GRANOLA

I threw this granola together once for a camping trip with what we had on hand, and have been making it since. It's very flexible in terms of what ingredients you use. I've tried a few different types of dried fruit in it, but my favourites are dried cranberries or, if I am feeling super fancy, blueberries. This particular version is nut-free, but chopped almonds and hazelnuts are very crunchy and delicious. If you aren't gluten-free and love oats as much as I do, you could substitute it for all or some of the buckwheat. Add any spices you like to jazz it up. You can sprinkle it over smoothie bowls, layer it in a brekkie parfait, or simply serve it with milk (I love oat, almond or coconut milk, page 178) or a generous dollop of yoghurt (I use coconut) along with some chopped fruit or stewed berries. So many options! Double or triple the recipe so you are all stocked up. I hope you love it as much as I do.

170 g (6 oz/2 cups) buckwheat kernels or oats

120 g (4½ oz/1 cup) dried fruit

70 g (2½ oz/½ cup) pumpkin seeds

65 g (2¼ oz/1½ cups) coconut chips

60 g (2 oz/½ cup) sunflower seeds

40 g (1½ oz/⅓ cup) sesame seeds

2 tablespoons flaxseeds (linseeds)

1 teaspoon cinnamon

1 teaspoon vanilla powder

3 tablespoons hulled tahini

2 tablespoons pure maple syrup

Preheat the oven to 180°C (350°F).

In a large mixing bowl, add all dry ingredients and stir until combined. Add the tahini and maple syrup and stir well.

Line the baking trays with baking paper and spread the mixture onto them evenly. Cook for 10 minutes. Remove the trays from the oven and gently stir the mixture, then return them to the oven for another 10 minutes, until it looks nice and toasted. Stir once more before putting them on cooling racks. Once the granola is fully cooled, store in an airtight container or jar in a cool, dry place for up to 3 weeks. The fresher, the better!

MAKES 250 ml (8½ fl oz/1 cup)

PREP TIME 5 minutes

EQUIPMENT high-speed blender or food processor + sterilised glass jar with lid

HEALTHY-MITE

Once you have tasted this easy-to-make, nutritionally dense version of that Aussie favourite, you will be hooked. It's high in calcium, magnesium, iron and B12 and made with only four ingredients; it's not hard to love something you can make in less than five minutes and that will last for the next two months. One of my absolute favourite ways to enjoy this spread is on the Oaty seed loaf (page 186) with avocado and beetroot Sauerkraut (page 175).

210 g (7½ oz/1½ cups) black sesame seeds

125 ml (4 fl oz/½ cup) coconut aminos

60 ml (2 fl oz/¼ cup) organic tamari

3 tablespoons nutritional yeast

Put all ingredients in a high-speed blender or food processor and pulse until the mixture becomes a smooth paste. Spoon it into a sterilised jar and store in the refrigerator. It will keep for up to 2 months.

CHOCOLATE SPREAD

MAKES 250 g (9 oz/1 cup)

PREP TIME 2 minutes

EQUIPMENT medium bowl, whisk, food processor (optional) + sterilised airtight glass jar

Spreadable chocolate: enough said! This plant-based version of a chocolate spread came about by accident when I wanted to make a choc spread but had no soaked nuts on hand. It couldn't be simpler; all you really need is your ingredients, a bowl and a whisk and you are good to go. Good luck sticking to using it as a delicious chocolate spread, though – it's just as good straight out of the jar with a spoon!

200 g (7 oz/¾ cup) hulled tahini

60 ml (2 fl oz/¼ cup) pure maple syrup

2 tablespoons cacao powder

pinch of salt

1 teaspoon vanilla powder or extract

In a medium bowl, whisk the tahini and maple syrup. Add all remaining ingredients and mix well. You can also do this in a food processor.

Transfer the spread to a clean glass jar and store in the refrigerator for up to 2 weeks.

CHOCOLATE
SPREAD

MAKES about 600 g (1 lb 5 oz/2 cups)

PREP TIME 1 hour 10 minutes (plus 12 hours soaking time)

EQUIPMENT large bowl, sieve, medium saucepan, mixing spoon, high-speed blender or food processor + airtight container

HUMMUS

Is there anything hummus doesn't go well with? We eat this delicious, hearty, versatile dip with SO many meals in our house. It is often the first thing I pull out of the fridge when friends arrive. I don't think any wrap or sandwich is complete without a spoonful! It has become increasingly popular, which means a staggering amount of supermarket versions wrapped in plastic packaging. But it's so easy to make at home with only a few ingredients, and nothing compares to fresh homemade hummus. The most arduous part is soaking the chickpeas, but the delayed gratification is totally worth it.

190 g (6½ oz/1 cup) dried chickpeas

750 ml (25½ fl oz/3 cups) filtered water

1 teaspoon good-quality salt

1 garlic clove, minced, or 3 teaspoons garlic powder

zest and juice of 3 lemons

60 ml (2 fl oz/¼ cup) hulled tahini

2 teaspoons ground cumin

125 ml (4 fl oz/½ cup) filtered water

OPTIONAL EXTRAS FOR FLAVOUR

1 roast capsicum + 1 teaspoon paprika

1 small steamed beetroot, chopped + 15 g (½ oz/¼ cup) fresh mint, chopped

Put the chickpeas in a large bowl, cover with the 3 cups filtered water and leave them to soak for 12 hours or overnight.

Once soaked, drain and rinse well. Put the chickpeas in a medium saucepan, then pour in enough filtered water to cover and add the salt. Stir a few times. Bring the chickpeas to the boil, then reduce to a simmer and let them cook for 1 hour.

Drain the chickpeas and allow them to cool to room temperature. Once cooled, add them to your food processor or high-speed blender with all remaining ingredients, including the ½ cup filtered water. Pulse everything a few times to combine, then blend until the hummus is super smooth.

Store in an airtight container in the refrigerator, where it will keep for 4 days.

INDEX

T

U

V

W

X

Y

Z

THANK YOU

A huge thank you to my friend and photographer Nikole Ramsay, who has brought these pages of words to life with her beautiful photography. All three books have been touched by her magic and incredible understanding of light. Collaborating with you is always a joy, with many a laugh along the way. And to Jade for your attention to detail and calming presence. It takes a village to create a book! Thank you to Bobby Alu for providing the happiest and cruisiest tunes to play on shoot days!

Thank you to my amazing publishing team at Hardie Grant. After self-publishing my first two books I did not know that there existed a publishing house that cared for quality and detail as much as Hardie Grant. Thank you to Jane Willson for trusting in not only this book but also in *Whole* and for taking us under your trusty wing. Thank you for your ongoing encouragement and positive energy through the entire process. Thank you to Loran McDougall for coordinating an epic team to take these images and text and bring it to life in a physical form; to Kate Armstrong for unjumbling my words; to Susanne Geppert, the typesetting extraordinaire; and to Bel Monypenny for proofreading to perfection.

Thank you to my surfing buddy and head recipe tester for *Home*, Carly, for your enthusiastic feedback and encouragement. Thank you to Clare, Jessie and Soph, my sounding-boards and cheerleaders for all three books. Thank you to Alex, who looked after the store while I was in a book burrow. Thank you to Maddie for your excitement and enthusiasm when it comes to anything Natural Harry related. Thank you to Katherine and Lynn at Valerie's Pantry for creating and running an amazing family-owned bulk wholefoods store. Thank you to all of my friends and family near and far for your constant encouragement. I do not thank you enough and I feel so lucky to have the biggest bunch of legends as my nearest and dearest!

Thank you to my husband, Fraser, for putting up with my turning our very small house into a testing ground for all things natural and DIY, food and otherwise, over the past seven years. Without you there would be no Natural Harry. Thank you for having my back and never discouraging me from doing what I love, even when it means big sacrifices.

Last but most definitely not least, thanks to YOU, whether this is your first Natural Harry book or your third. I would like to thank you for your support, for sharing your love of the books and for your encouragement along the way. From my home to yours, I hope your copy is used and treasured for years to come.

ABOUT THE AUTHOR

Harriet Birrell is an authentic woman on a mission to show people how easy (and fulfilling!) it can be to reduce waste and live a cleaner, tox-free life. Harriet is a qualified holistic health coach and yoga teacher, and has studied plant-based nutrition at e-Cornell University.

Harriet started her food journey serving organic smoothies and raw desserts from a caravan on a bush block in the coastal town of Barwon Heads on Victoria's Bellarine Peninsula. This led to her first book, *Natural Harry*, the success of which she followed with *Whole* (driven by her equally passionate mission to celebrate the abundance of colourful whole plant-based recipes).

When she is not cooking, or surfing, or tending her veggie patch with dog Fred by her side, she is busy working on her blog, hosting workshops and creating content, as well as running her online store, a thoughtful and considered collection of ever-changing small-batch collaboration products.

This edition published in 2026 by Hardie Grant Books, an imprint of Hardie Grant Publishing
First published in 2020

Hardie Grant Books (Melbourne)
Wurundjeri Country
Level 11, 36 Wellington Street
Collingwood, Victoria 3066

Hardie Grant North America
2912 Telegraph Ave
Berkeley, California 94705

hardiegrant.com/books

Hardie Grant acknowledges the Traditional Owners of the Country on which we work, the Wurundjeri People of the Kulin Nation and the Gadigal People of the Eora Nation, and recognises their continuing connection to the land, waters and culture. We pay our respects to their Elders past and present.

A catalogue record for this book is available from the National Library of Australia

Home: DIY Recipes for a Toxin-Free, Low-Waste Life
ISBN 978 1 76145 188 1
ISBN 978 1 76144 401 2 (ebook)

10 9 8 7 6 5 4 3 2 1

Publishing Director: Jane Willson
Project Editor: Loran McDougall
Editor: Kate J. Armstrong
Creative Director: Kristin Thomas
Designer: Celia Mance
Photographer: Nikole Ramsay
Illustrator: Ngaio Parr
Production Manager: Todd Rechner
Production Controller: Elly Cridland

Colour reproduction by Splitting Image Colour Studio
Printed in China by Leo Paper Products LTD.

The paper this book is printed on is from FSC®-certified forests and other sources. FSC® promotes environmentally responsible, socially beneficial and economically viable management of the world's forests.